THE SHORT-SEA ROUTE

DOVER

CALAIS

John Hendy

Published by:
Ferry Publications, PO Box 33, Ramsey, Isle of Man IM99 4LP
Tel: +44 (0) 1624 898446   Fax: +44 (0) 1624 898449
E-mail: FerryPubs@manx.net   Website: www.ferrypubs.co.uk

FERRY
Publications

© Ferry Publications 2009

Published by Lily Publications Ltd on behalf of Ferry Publications

Produced and designed by Lily Publications Ltd

Printed in Wales at Gomer Press Ltd

*The **Free Enterprise II** (Captain D Bruce) alongside the **Dover** for refit in the Wellington Dock in 1967. (AG Jones)*

INTRODUCTION

THE SHORT-SEA ROUTE

The twenty-two miles that span the narrow seas between Dover and Calais are the most intensively operated sea route in the world. The ports' favoured geographical positions, facing each other across the Dover Strait, have seen a phenomenal growth in traffic in the last forty years which even the opening of the Channel Tunnel has failed to assuage.

The fact that both ports are so conveniently situated did not automatically mean that their success was assured. There have been periods when the local townsmen have been required to struggle and fight against the physical forces which continue to pose a threat to their very existence.

The North Downs, the spine of Kent, finally reach the English Channel east of Folkestone where erosion by the sea has formed the famed White Cliffs of Dover. Proceeding eastwards beyond Dover and around the South Foreland to Deal, the chalk dips ever lower disappearing from sight by Kingsdown and under Pegwell Bay before rising briefly again to form the Isle of Thanet. Thus along some twelve miles of coastline, the vertical wall of chalk presents not only a secure bastion against would-be invaders but also a most inhospitable environment in which to build a port.

Fortunately there is one place where the White Cliffs are breached. At this place the River Dour and its once numerous tributaries, swollen by the melting snows of the last ice age, washed out a series of broad-based valleys in and around where modern day Dover today stands. Observing this dribbling stream today, it is difficult to imagine that the Dour was ever capable of such a feat but up its wide estuary the Romans sailed their galleys and their quays have been discovered beneath the town's Market Square.

During the Middle Ages there was a flourishing shipbuilding industry on the east bank of the estuary and as Dover was the only legitimate exit from the country, those ships were kept busy plying the narrow neck of the Dover Strait.

Until the present harbour was completed, the greatest problem facing the port was the relentless easterly movement of shingle along the coast which continually choked the river and early harbour entrances.

For approximately 300 days a year, the prevailing wind is from the south west quarter and all along the south coast of England, the wind-blown waves strike the coast at an angle and cause what is known as longshore drift.

After gales and storms, when more shingle than usual would be thrown across the harbour mouth, low tides would see gangs of men busy with shovels attempting to remove the tons of pebbles in order that enough deep water might be created for boats to use the port on the next high tide. Horse-drawn carts would then carry the excavated shingle to the high-water mark thus helping to protect the town from the future ravages of the sea.

In the reign of Elizabeth I, an ingenious scheme was devised with the construction of a wet dock with a sluice which would be allowed to fill with water as the tide came in. At the top of the tide, the sluice was closed thereby keeping the water pent-up inside. As the tide ebbed, the trapped water in the Pent (as the basin became known) was released thereby washing away the shingle across the harbour mouth. This was a simple and fairly successful solution to an age-old problem but by the nineteenth century, something more radical was called for.

In 1836 a Parliamentary Inquiry was set up which brought the local problems of a small Kentish town to those of national level and from which the massive harbour we know today was created.

As far as crossing the Channel at its narrowest point was concerned, it was left to the local boat owners to provide whatever service was required. Foreign letters were made up into 'packets' and the term 'packet boat' was used to describe the vessels that carried them. These boats were small, about 40 tons, and most managed to cross to or from France on a single tide. However, if the tide was missed the boat was forced to lay-by and passengers in their frustration at seeing the shore just a few yards away would often pay local watermen large sums of money to bodily carry them ashore. The famous 'Punch' cartoon showing such a scene and with the waterman saying, 'Five bob (25p) or I drops yer!' was all too true.

Calais too was faced with problems. Whereas Dover lay in a river valley which had been cut through the chalk cliffs to form a natural estuary, the French port is situated well east of the chalk ridge where the flat plain of Picardy is protected from the sea by a tall ridge of sand dunes, a feature which continues along the coast past Dunkirk and across the border into Belgium and Holland. The narrow entrance of Calais Harbour was notorious during the Victorian era and there are many instances where the fast-flowing tides swept slow-manoeuvring paddle steamers onto the sands where they were stranded until the next high water.

The city was besieged and captured by the forces of King Edward III in 1347 and remained in English hands until 1558. During this period it even sent its own representatives to the Houses of Parliament in London when it was known as 'the brightest jewel in the English crown'.

The ties between the two ports have always been strong and continue to be so today with the stretch of water linking them, the world's most intensively operated short-sea crossing.

John Hendy
Ivychurch
Romney Marsh
Kent

A classic out-of-season 1950s scene of the **Isle of Thanet** *alongside the Dover - Dunkirk train ferry* **Shepperton Ferry** *in the Wellington Dock at Dover. (John Hendy collection)*

CHAPTER ONE

EARLY DAYS: THE BEGINNING OF STEAM

PIONEERING STEAMSHIPS

The first crossing to Calais by steamship occurred as early as 1816 when the 39-ton *Margery* 'with two hundred courageous passengers' arrived at the port. The vessel had been built at Dumbarton in 1814 for a Mr. W. Anderson who had named her after his daughter. He later sold the ship to a Mr. Curtis and she made the passage to London via the Forth & Clyde Canal, becoming the first steamship to be seen in southern English waters, apparently to the dismay of those on board several naval vessels who had never previously seen such a vessel. The *Margery* had been acquired in order to operate a service between London and the developing seaside resort of Margate but in 1816 was sent to France to run on the River Seine, hence her epic crossing of the Channel to Calais.

However, the first regular steamship service between Dover and Calais commenced in 1821 using the steamer *Rob Roy*. As her name indicates, she was also Scottish in origin being built at Dumbarton in 1818 for the famous Scottish engineer William Napier. What was special about the tiny 81 ft. long steamer was that she was the first in the world designed for service in the open sea in any weather. She was first used on the Glasgow – Belfast service but was later purchased by a Mr. Boyd and arrived at Dover on 10th June 1821 commencing her daily crossings to Calais five days later.

It is not surprising that the public were initially very wary of the new

*The **Arrow** was built for the Post Office in 1821 but renamed **Ariel** when the service was taken over by the Admiralty in 1837. She is seen arriving in February 1840 with Prince Albert on board, prior to his wedding to Queen Victoria. (John Hendy collection)*

vessel that made strange noises and ejected vast amounts of black smoke but the *Rob Roy* did not take long to prove herself. Indeed, there were occasions when so many passengers were on offer that the Captain had to promise to return for them on a second trip. Should the tide be missed at Calais, the steamer would be forced to wait until the next or call upon the longboats of the local pilotage service to rescue the stranded passengers who then were forced to climb steep and slippery ladders up the harbour walls in order to reach the adjacent quayside.

*Seen in the Wellington Dock at Dover, the London Chatham & Dover Railway's **Prince Imperial** was built for the French mail contract in 1864 but was renamed **Prince** in 1872. At 327 gross tons, the clipper bowed steamer was typical of the Dover - Calais ships of this period. On the right is the cargo steamer **Chatham**. (South Eastern & Chatham Railway Society)*

*A picture full of interest and showing laid-up units of the London Chatham & Dover Railway's fleet. In the Wellington Dock (foreground) are the clipper-bowed **Prince**, the sisters **Foam** and **Wave** and the much larger **Invicta**. On the Cross Wall in the Granville Dock is the double-hulled **Calais-Douvres**. (John Hendy collection)*

That same month, the Post Office ordered their own vessels *Dasher* and *Arrow* the first taking only four months to build on the Thames.

The French Postal Administration purchased the *Rob Roy* in 1822 and renamed her *Henri Quatre*. Very soon other small steamers entered service, some being built at Dover for local owners, and the days of the sailing vessels were numbered. Interestingly, the early steamers took about 3 hours 30 minutes for the passage, which was about the same time as their sailing counterparts, but they had the advantage of consistency and the ability to cross the Strait no matter from which quarter the wind blew.

The Admiralty took over the operation of the packet boats in April 1837, renaming and repainting five former Post Office ships (*Arrow, Firefly, Crusader, Ferret* and *Salamander*) and inviting the crews to signup on naval terms. In poor weather when they were unable to berth at Dover, the packets would be offloaded at Margate or Deal from where the precious mails would be sent on to London via Canterbury. These early steamers were not very dependable and there were often two or three off service at the same time undergoing engine repairs. At these times, emergency arrangements were required and local sailing smacks were hired to maintain the service.

An attempt to list these numerous small early steam vessels has been made in the Fleet Lists (page 113). Many of the locally owned fleets, and those belonging to both the Post Office and to the Admiralty, led extremely peripatetic careers being used on a variety of routes and were not always linked to the Dover – Calais service.

THE SOUTH EASTERN RAILWAY

The long-awaited arrival of the South Eastern Railway (SER) was greeted at Folkestone in June 1843 when the line reached the town via Reigate, Tonbridge and Ashford. A regular steamship service to Boulogne almost immediately followed on 1st August thereby allowing passengers to reach London from Boulogne in just six hours.

At this time the SER was not permitted to operate its own steamers and so unsatisfactory (and unreliable) chartering arrangements were made. So unhappy were the directors of the line that in 1845 they formed the South Eastern & Continental Steam Packet Company to operate ships on their behalf from Folkestone to Boulogne and also from Dover to Ostend, Boulogne and Calais. It was not for another eight years that the SER gained the necessary parliamentary permission to operate its own steamers.

Previously the SER had extended its line along the base of the chalk cliffs, through the Warren and onto Dover where amid great ceremony, the first train arrived in February 1844.

On the French side, the railway network was slower to develop and although Boulogne was finally linked to Paris in 1851, the station was in the town centre and still some way from the steamer berths. This was a boom time for the Folkestone – Boulogne route when passengers preferred it to the Dover – Calais crossing as although the crossing was shorter, the Paris to Calais rail link was inland via Lille and consequently took much longer. Thus, until the Boulogne to Calais railway line was completed in 1867, at which time the Dover – Calais link was able to assert itself once again by offering a direct service with Paris, Dover continued to lose out heavily.

During the period between 1848 and 1862, the SER steamers continued to offer a daily tidal service between Dover and Calais and return. Leaving Dover at between 05.00 and midday, their return was

*The double-hulled **Castalia** berthed on the Cross Wall in the Granville Dock. Notice the open bridge between the funnels. In the distance, the Lord Warden Hotel is connected by an overhead walkway to Dover Town station. (John Hendy collection)*

timed between the hours of 04.00 and 14.30. The Admiralty's mail (packet) boats, however, ran to a fixed timetable leaving Dover at 14.15 and 23.00 and returning from Calais at 03.00 and 21.40.

The Admiralty's operation of the mail contract became far from satisfactory and so in 1853, WE Gladstone (then Chancellor of the Exchequer) sought to save £10,000 a year by putting it out to tender. Messrs Jenkins & Churchward of Dover won the contract and their vessel *John Penn* crossed from Dover to Calais during 1859 in a record time of 1 hour 23 minutes.

THE LONDON CHATHAM & DOVER RAILWAY

During its existence the SER had witnessed the formation of a number of independent Kentish railway schemes before they ran out of finance at which time the established company had acted quickly to absorb and add them to a growing network.

The East Kent Railway looked like being another brave enterprise to end up under the South Eastern's growing wing but much to its consternation, the 'upstart' continued from Strood to Faversham and joined up with smaller concerns to gain a London terminus before pushing on from Canterbury across the North Downs to Dover in July 1861.

By this time it had grandly titled itself the London Chatham & Dover Railway (LC&DR) and what has been termed, 'the forty years railway war' broke out with the SER. This resulted in many hare-brained schemes in order to capture traffic from each other but which only served to make the financial positions of each company even more precarious than otherwise. Eventually, both saw sense and formed a working union on New Year's Day 1899.

If the LC&DR provided a railway service that was the target of many a Victorian music hall performer, their marine section was second to none and an extraordinarily fine service was created.

At Dover, the Admiralty Pier was under construction at this time and Continental Expresses from both the SER and LC&DR competed for traffic, rival trains racing each other for access to the new pier with the LC&DR approaching from the direction of Dover Priory station while the SER expresses reached the Admiralty Pier from their coastal main line.

As a result of a tremendous amount of parliamentary wrangling, the local ship owners Jenkins & Churchward lost the English mail contract in 1862 when the *Ondine*, *Garland* and *Prince Frederick William* passed to the railway company. As the contractor for the Dover – Calais mail

*The **Calais-Douvres** at sea. During her brief career she certainly made crossings more comfortable but was uneconomical to operate during the winter months when she was most required. (John Hendy collection)*

The **Invicta** of 1882 is seen leaving the Admiralty Pier late in her career when she was on charter to the Nord Railway of France. The open nature of the pier made life difficult in SW gales. (John Hendy collection)

The **Victoria** of 1886 was a product of the Fairfield yard at Govan. Her stem-like stern for ease of leaving Calais should be noted. (John Hendy collection)

*The **Dover** of 1896 was the first of a trio of sister ships built by Denny of Dumbarton mainly for the night service. (John Hendy collection)*

service, Churchward continued for a while but as from 1863, the South Eastern's trains carried the mails from London to Dover while the LC&DR's ships carried them to Calais. The South Eastern had earlier retired its ships from Dover and concentrated all future cross-Channel efforts from their own port at Folkestone. The year 1862 had also seen the Dover – Ostend service entirely in the hands of the Belgian Marine.

The great advantages of the new Admiralty Pier (where in those early days, ships could berth on either side) were obvious. Trains could now draw up alongside the ships frequently saving long delays while passengers and their huge amounts of baggage were transferred from the town's original stations in horse-drawn carts. Secondly, the pier acted as a giant groyne and now saved the port from being choked with shingle while thirdly, it allowed a fixed service to be operated as its deep-water berths were not subject to the same crippling restrictions of the former tidal sailings.

However, across the Strait at Calais matters remained as bad as ever

with passengers only able to land on either side of high water. During low tides, the tender *Poste* was used to ferry passengers ashore.

It was not until 1864 that the LC&DR gained permission to operate its own steamers and in the meantime, Jenkins & Churchward worked the Dover to Calais passage on their behalf. There was an urgent need for new tonnage and so the first two of a very successful class of ship were constructed on the Thames and entered service in March 1862. These were the *Samphire* (after which the class was named) and the *Maid of Kent* which were each of about 365 gross tons and the first ships on the route to be fitted with private cabins for the night service on which it was planned they would operate. The *Samphire* made record crossings during her trials in May 1862 crossing to Calais in 83 minutes and returning to Dover in just 78 minutes.

As soon as the LC&DR had gained the necessary parliamentary permission to run the Dover – Calais mail service itself, the older ships were quickly disposed of and more of the *Samphire* class were introduced in the form of the *Petrel* (the first Dover ship to have an all steel hull), *Breeze* and *Wave* along with the larger *Foam* and *Scud*.

The *Petrel*, *Foam* and *Scud* proved somewhat embarrassing for the LC&DR. Seizing on another opportunity to outdo its rival concern, it was their intention to work the ships on the Dover - Boulogne route, their larger size making them ideal for Boulogne but quite unsuitable for Calais.

The Nord Railway of France then became involved and refused to allow the rival English railway companies to take their 'railway war' into its ports thereby keeping the operations of Folkestone – Boulogne and Dover – Calais quite separate from each other. With three new ships having to spend their time in reserve, charter work was sought and in 1893 the *Scud* enjoyed a rare period of employment with Belgian Marine on their Ostend – Dover route.

The French had taken over the running of their own mails in 1862 and, deprived of the right to operate the English mails, Jenkins & Churchward operated it for them using initially the old *Queen* and

*Dover Admiralty Pier in about 1900 during the construction of its extension. One of the 1896 **Dover** class has just arrived at the outside berth while a sister vessel lies on the east side of the pier. The two-funnelled vessel further away is one of the 'Ostenders'. (John Hendy collection)*

*The **Empress** of 1887 was fitted with an enclosed wheelhouse forward of the funnels. The ship is already well under way in this illustration. (John Hendy collection)*

Empress but soon building the clipper-bowed *Prince Imperial* (later renamed *Prince*) and *La France* both of which were able to cross the Strait in 1 hour 25 minutes on a good tide.

The Franco-Prussian War in 1870 naturally saw a sharp reduction in the services across the narrow seas but the Prussian advance did not reach either Calais or Boulogne and in any case, all mails were re-routed via Ostend.

With the French day mail contract expiring in 1872, the new Government decreed that in future the French themselves must carry the mail to England and put the contract up for tender. It was duly won by two journalists who immediately sought suitable tonnage with which to operate their new service. With nothing available, three old, small and very slow gunboats were duly acquired for duty – the *Auverne*, *Faon* and *Vigie*. Although they were later replaced, this greatly outraged the LC&DR who had prided themselves on a fast and efficient service and not surprisingly, much traffic was lost to the SER's rival Folkestone – Boulogne route. The whole situation became even more farcical when following a breakdown to one of its vessels, the new French company was forced to charter the *Palmerston*; a Dover Harbour Board tug. Matters did improve after more suitable ships were found (the former Belgian packets *Diamant* and *Perle*) but even these were both ancient and too small and it was not surprising when in 1873, the French swallowed their national pride and handed the service to the LC&DR.

DEFEATING MAL DE MER

One of the most remarkable periods of the route's history concerned three of the strangest ships ever to be constructed for any of the cross-Channel links.

The Dover – Calais service, although the shortest, could also be one of the most uncomfortable as the route, crossing the Dover Strait at right angles was and is subject to unusually strong tidal movements as the water in the North Sea and the wider English Channel surges through the narrow neck between the two ports. As already observed, entering Calais at reduced speed during a fast tidal flow brought many a Channel steamer to a premature landfall when the passengers would have to wait until low tide and walk ashore across the sands. But it was usually the pier heads at the French port that came in for most of the battering.

The first of these strange vessels was the *Castalia* which was built at Thames Ironworks and named after Lady Granville who launched the ship in June 1874. The ship was the brainchild of a Captain Dicey and was basically a catamaran with two half-hulls linked by girders between which were the paddles. For many years Dicey had been Harbour Master

at the port of Calcutta and had become aware the stability of the local native canoes and catamarans.

His new vessel was at that time the largest Channel ship ever built measuring some 290 ft by 60 ft with a gross tonnage of 1,553. In her unusually wide beam lay what Captain Dicey hoped would be the answer to the problem which beset all those who sailed the narrow seas in small ships: sea sickness – mal de mer. The stability of the *Castalia* would, it was believed, make for a comfortable passage for up to 700 passengers and because Calais harbour was so difficult, the ship was double-ended and would not therefore require turning at the commencement of the return trip to Dover.

Although the *Castalia* was owned by the English Channel Steamship Company, the LC&DR certainly encouraged them and were keen to monitor the new ship's performance. She arrived at Dover during October 1874 but after repairs to her boilers sailed again to London in the following month where new boilers and paddles were fitted, her speed on trials failing disastrously to live up to expectations.

The following June, the *Castalia* was back at Dover and crossing to Calais for the first time. Enough encouragement was forthcoming to commence a regular timetable in competition with the railway company from early August. Unfortunately she was still too slow and passengers crossing in her from Dover frequently found that their trains at Calais had already left. The ship also proved extremely costly to operate and although new paddle floats were fitted early in 1877, her owners were bankrupt and after being sold in 1883, the sad ship ended her days as a smallpox isolation hospital for infectious diseases in Long Reach near Dartford on the Thames. There she was fitted with five ward blocks making her resemble a floating street rather than a ship.

The second of the Victorian oddities was Henry Bessemer's *Bessemer*. The great inventor will ever be associated with his converter that changed iron into steel but towards the end of his productive life, spent much time and energy working on steamship design. As he suffered badly from sea-sickness, his new ship would, he hoped, alleviate the problem as his plan was based on building a ship which was so long that she could not pitch fore and aft. The *Bessemer* was again a double-ended ship with two pairs of paddles but with only a single hull, her claim to fame being that she was designed with a hanging saloon measuring 70 ft by 35 ft. This would be operated by a hydraulic apparatus which was controlled by one of the seamen, the complete structure resting on a large rubber bed in order to prevent vibration.

The *Bessemer*, designed by E.J. Read on the principal invented by Henry Bessemer, was built at Hull and again suffered from a lack of

In 1898, the Nord Railway introduced the **Le Nord** *and* **Le Pas de Calais**, *the largest paddle steamers ever built for the link. Here one of the sisters is captured heading up through the jetties at Calais. (John Hendy collection)*

speed, only 11 knots being managed instead of the intended 20. The £40,000 ship's first Calais crossing was from Gravesend in April 1875 but on arrival in the French port she smashed into the pier damaging both it and herself. While repairs were being carried out in Dover's Granville Dock, the public were invited to view her and were charged 1/- (5p) for the privilege.

The ship was out again in early May and once more crossed to Calais when the attraction of the pier proved too much and more damage was caused. Modifications and a great deal of sprucing up were then carried out in readiness for a special VIP sailing later that month which proved to be a public relations nightmare. The ship crossed in a very commendable time of 90 minutes but entered Calais as the tide was sweeping through the pier heads, failed to answer the helm and took away 50 ft of the west pier. Eventually extricating herself, she then collided with the east pier before the red-faced VIPs finally disembarked.

The *Bessemer's* saloon was never tested and the ship was a costly failure. She was laid up and eventually sold to a Hull company who rebuilt her and removed the swinging saloon which was brought ashore and used as a billiard room in a Kentish garden. The ship was sold for scrap in 1877.

The third ship was a modified *Castalia* and a further product of Captain Dicey and his renamed English Channel Transit Company. She was launched on the River Tyne in April 1877 and named *Express*. The vessel had two complete hulls and far more powerful engines but it was not long before her owners experienced financial problems and the ship was promptly purchased by the LC&DR who renamed her *Calais – Douvres*.

Completing her maiden voyage in the month after her launch, she was without doubt the most successful of the three 'oddities' and appears to have been very much liked by passengers. The 'Dover Express'

reported in February 1879:

'The running between Dover and Calais of the *Calais-Douvres* during the past season appears to have justified expectation. She performed the trip with great regularity, making good and quick passages. There was a great increase in comfort and considerable reduction in the incidence of sea-sickness.

During the season, upwards of 55,000 passengers crossed in her, or an average of 715 a day, a number which on many occasions would have involved the necessity of running two of the ordinary mail boats.

This may be regarded as in some measure a set-off against the unquestionably heavy cost of working a ship of the size and capacity of the *Calais-Douvres*'.

Using some 40 tons of coal a day, she was certainly expensive to operate and at only 13 knots found it difficult to maintain the demanding schedules expected of the LC&DR's mail ships. She became increasingly uneconomic to operate in the winter months when traffic levels fell off

A view from the Lord Warden Hotel showing the newly opened Marine Station. Either the **Le Nord** *or* **Le Pas de Calais** *is alongside. (John Hendy collection)*

but at which times she was most needed to prove herself.

The *Calais-Douvres* was finally withdrawn from service in 1887 and ended her days as a coal hulk on the Thames.

Never again were a series of such strange ships built for any cross-Channel route but their eccentric designs encapsulated the spirit and confidence of the age when it was believed that the great Victorian engineers could do little wrong. The failure of the trio was a bitter blow but there are those who would argue that, just as with Brunel's *Great Eastern,* they were, perhaps years ahead of their time.

Following their foray into the technological unknown, the LC&DR now ordered four magnificent paddle steamers of conventional design save for stem-like sterns for ease of coming astern out of Calais. All four ships were of about 1,100 gross tons, the first being the *Invicta* of 1882, the last Dover ship to be built on the Thames and the first to be lit entirely of electricity. The name 'Invicta' means 'undaunted' and is the motto of the county of Kent which was also adopted by the LC&DR.

The other three ships all differed slightly but were products of the Fairfield yard on the Clyde: the *Victoria* of 1886, the *Empress* of 1887 and the second named *Calais-Douvres* of 1889 which was ordered to assist with the anticipated traffic which the 1889 Paris Exhibition was expected to generate. Shortly after entering service, on 21st June 1887, the *Empress* became the first cross-Channel steamer to make the crossing to Calais in an hour.

Although very comfortable and successful steamers, none of the quartet was to show her true potential due to two unforeseen events. The amalgamation of the two rival Kentish railway companies in 1899 and the introduction of the steam turbine which virtually brought about the end of the British paddle steamer era within a decade of the introduction of the first ship of the new class.

In the early 1890s, work at last started on widening and deepening Calais Harbour but until this was completed in 1895, the services were again required of some of the small 1860s vessels of the *Samphire* class which had proved to be so reliable and economical for so many years until they were finally disposed of at the turn of the century. The public, however, were not impressed and expecting more modern and larger ships, turned again to the patronage of the South Eastern Railway's Folkestone – Boulogne route.

With dredging at Calais completed in 1895, the large steamers were now able to berth there at any state of the tide and in the following year, the LC&DR turned to Denny's of Dumbarton to supply the twin night service sister ships *Dover* and *Calais* thereby helping Dover to once again assert its authority. Their success prompted the order of a third sister, the *Lord Warden.*

Now that Calais could claim to be a modern port, in 1896 the French once more decided to operate their own mails and the Nord Railway ordered two ships from Ateliers et Chantiers de la Loire at St. Nazaire. Until they were ready two years later, the English vessels *Invicta, Victoria* and the smaller *Petrel* and *Foam* were transferred to French management.

With the appearance of the new *Le Nord* and *Le Pas de Calais,* the older ships were disposed of and for the first time the Chemin de Fer du Nord could boast of two new and worthy vessels which were more than capable of holding their own against their English counterparts. Not only were they the largest cross-Channel paddle steamers ever built, at 2,004 gross tons, but they were also the only paddle steamers built in France for this particular type of service.

Both ships also laid claim to fame in that they sank submarines; *Le Pas de Calais* accidentally ramming the French vessel *Pluviose* which surfaced ahead of her in May 1910 and her sister, deliberately sinking a German U-boat when serving as a seaplane carrier during the Great War.

The end came for the **Le Nord** *in May 1923 when in fog, she missed the entrance of Dover Harbour and ran aground on the rocks below the South Foreland. (John Hendy collection)*

CHAPTER TWO

THE TURBINE STEAMERS: 60-MINUTE CROSSINGS

AMALGAMATION AND THE SE&CR

The 'forty years railway war' finally came to an end on New Year's Day 1899 when the South Eastern Railway and the London Chatham & Dover Railway formed the South Eastern & Chatham Railways Joint Managing Committee, the former SER taking a 60% share with the LC&DR the other 40%. The new company was commonly known as the South Eastern & Chatham Railway (SE&CR) and a joint fleet of 25 ships was created; 12 former South Eastern ships from the Folkestone – Boulogne route and 13 London Chatham & Dover vessels from the Dover – Calais link.

Now for the first time the prime units were tried on each other's routes while much of the older tonnage was soon disposed of. Instead of wasting much time, energy and finance competing unsuccessfully with each other, the Working Union created perhaps the most powerful and splendid looking fleet of cross-Channel steamers ever to be based in one port.

Dover Harbour continued to expand to meet the demand and rise in traffic although its prime purpose was to house the Channel Fleet. With this in mind, the Admiralty Pier was extended between 1897 – 1907, the Prince of Wales Pier was built between 1892 – 1902 while the Eastern Arm and then the Southern Breakwater were finally completed in 1909. Between 1909 and 1913 the Admiralty Pier was widened with the infilling of a large area immediately to the east of the original pier but by the time that the great new Marine Station was ready for use, war had broken out.

Following the outstanding success of two turbine driven excursion steamers on the River Clyde, the famous Dumbarton shipbuilders Wm. Denny & Bros. suggested to the SE&CR that a similar vessel for use in the Channel might prove of great benefit. Work was immediately started and in April 1903 the elegant turbine steamer *The Queen* slid down the ways into the River Leven. When she entered service on 29th June, the 21-knot ship became an immediate success and prompted her proud owners to introduce the similar *Onward* and *Invicta* in 1905 (mottos on the coats of arms of the former SER and LC&DR) and the *Empress* and

The premier turbine steamer **The Queen** *is seen alongside the Admiralty Pier early in her career. The Continental Boat Express (led by D class number 730) is drawn up alongside her. Notice the portholes in the turbine's forward superstructure; the other four of the class had windows in this position. (John Hendy collection)*

*The penultimate turbine steamer in the initial quintet was the **Victoria** of 1907, seen on trials in the Firth of Clyde. In 1928 she was sold to the Isle of Man Steam Packet Company and was not scrapped until 1957. (John Hendy collection)*

Victoria in 1907.

Such was their performance that the paddle steamers were rendered redundant and were sold or retired for 'stand-by' duties.

The five new steamers measured 323 ft x 40 ft, were each of about 1,600 gross tons and were two class vessels; First Class forward, Second Class aft. *The Queen* was fitted with no fewer than five screws when new although this was soon reduced to the triple-screw arrangement.

The five new ships worked both routes from Dover to Calais and Folkestone to Boulogne although *The Queen* and the *Onward* were mainly associated with the latter service following the delivery of the *Victoria* in June 1907.

Further orders were made and in 1911 the splendid *Rivieria* and *Engadine* appeared replacing the last of the British paddlers. A sign of the times was their specially strengthened awning decks for the carriage of motor cars.

It is difficult to appreciate, largely because the economics of such an operation would be impossible today, that these ships were only in service for two or three months before they retired to the Wellington or

*The cargo vessel **Walmer** is seen alongside the Continental Cargo Shed in May 1927. She was built as the **Trouville** in 1894 for the Newhaven - Caen service but was sold with her sister ships to the SE&CR in 1901. (AE Glen)*

Granville Docks at Dover for overhaul and repainting. Mostly they were required to operate just one return sailing each day and if any particular crossing looked as if it might be heavily booked, a reserve steamer was hastily brought in to offer a duplicate sailing. The ships each had one crew (a state of affairs that existed until the introduction of the Dover – Dunkirk train ferries in 1936), who lived and ate ashore and pride and purpose were very evident.

Shortly before the outbreak of war in 1914, two more turbines were ordered from Denny's Dumbarton yard although neither took up civilian service until 1920. As the *Biarritz* (1915) and *Maid of Orleans* (1918) they represented the final flowering of the class and were, in the opinion of this writer, the most magnificent cross-Channel steamers ever built for the short-sea routes. Their lines were perfect with superb flair and sheer, and twin funnels and masts of just the right proportions and rake. Trial speeds of almost 24 knots were attained which made them the fastest turbines ever to operate on the Dover – Calais service.

The First World War saw *The Queen* and the *Onward* lost. The former was intercepted and sunk by a German flotilla off the Varne Bank in August 1916 while the *Onward* caught fire and capsized while alongside at Folkestone in September 1918. She was raised in a unique salvage operation and hauled upright by the collective power of five steam locomotives. Following a refit on the Thames, she was sold to the Isle of Man Steam Packet Company and as the *Mona's Isle* (IV), was not broken up until 1948.

On New Year's Day 1923, all 120 British railway companies were grouped into the 'Big Four' – the London & North Eastern Railway (LNER), the London Midland and Scottish Railway (LMS), the Great Western Railway (GWR) and the Southern Railway (SR). The new Southern Railway Company absorbed the South Eastern & Chatham Railway and the black funnels, which the fleet had worn since the end of the war, were repainted buff with black tops.

In June 1920, the Chemin de Fer du Nord had sold their paddle

*With a full head of steam, the turbine steamer **Invicta** pulls away from the Admiralty Pier early in her career. (John Hendy collection)*

*The SE&CR's second set of turbine steamers were the **Riviera** and **Engadine** of 1911 which were constructed with stronger awning decks for the carriage of motor cars. Here is the **Engadine** on trials in the Firth of Clyde. (John Hendy collection)*

*HMS **Biarritz** is seen leaving the Grand Harbour in Valetta, Malta, during the First World War. As a mine-layer, she was responsible for the sinking of the German cruiser **Breslau** and damaging the battle cruiser **Goeben**. (Imperial War Museum)*

*Sister to the **Biarritz** was the first **Maid of Orleans** which is seen approaching Dover at speed under the command of Captain RE Carey in about 1921. She is wearing the post-war black funnelled livery of the SE&CR; her classic lines have never been bettered. (John Hendy collection)*

The view looking astern along the Boat Deck of the **Maid of Orleans** *swinging in Dover Harbour shortly after the First World War. (John Hendy collection)*

steamers *Le Nord* and *Le Pas de Calais* to the Societe Anonyme de Gerance et d'Armement (SAGA). Until 1923, the ships continued to maintain the morning mail service from Calais but the pending introduction of new English tonnage simply served to highlight the age difference and technological advances between them and there was no doubt that the French badly needed to update their vessels on the premier link. They were given a helping hand when in May 1923, on a particularly foggy morning the *Le Nord* had the misfortune to miss the entrance of Dover Harbour and run ashore on rocks below the South Foreland. With her elderly hull badly damaged, the new Southern Railway stepped in and offered the French the turbine steamers *Empress* (1907) and *Invicta* (1905) which duly passed to French ownership in June and August that year. The improvements in passenger comforts brought about by the introduction of the Southern's *Isle of Thanet* were soon followed by SAGA who plated in the open promenade decks of their new ships and also repainted their funnels white. The *Invicta* and *Empress* lasted for a further ten years before they were replaced by two splendid new additions.

THE SOUTHERN RAILWAY AND THE 'GOLDEN ARROW'

The first ships built for the Southern Railway were the *Isle of Thanet* and *Maid of Kent* which entered service in July and November 1925. They

were certainly needed as following the end of the Great War, the tremendous boom in Continental travel imposed a huge strain on the existing steamers. Whereas in the early years of the century most passengers' luggage was too bulky to hand-hold and was loaded directly into the ships' holds, it was found that increasing numbers of travellers now seemed to make it a point of honour to overload themselves with so much hand luggage that the passenger decks became hopelessly cluttered. It was time for a total reappraisal of the basic design of the cross-Channel steamer and so the new 'Isle' and 'Maid' were very much revolutionary ships.

The open promenade decks were discontinued, the whole of the ships' sides being plated in and far more enclosed than previously, cabins were placed down the centre line of the ships and altogether far more covered space was provided, much more room being available to the designers through concentrating the boiler uptakes into one funnel. The new ships carried 1,400 passengers with as many as 1,000 in the First Class.

Not only did the new twins differ in the matters previously outlined but they introduced cruiser sterns which replaced the fine counter sterns of the previous steamers. As can be seen from the illustrations, the counter stern was extremely elegant but was very prone to damage when

*A c1920 view of the **Engadine** and one of the earlier turbine steamers laid up on the Cross Wall in the Granville Dock with the Dover Harbour Board's tug, **Lady Brassey** also in attendance. The cargo steamer **CW Eborall** lies on the West Quay by the Continental Goods Shed in front of the Lord Warden Hotel. (John Hendy collection)*

berthing stern first, as was the practice, when at high water the overhanging counter could override the quay.

The last of the original SE&CR quintet of turbine steamers to remain in service at Dover was the *Victoria*, or 'The Old Vic' as she became affectionately known. However, in March 1928 she followed her sister ship the *Onward* and passed into the ownership of the Isle of Man Steam Packet Company for whom she survived, without a change of name, until 1956 when she was broken up. It had been a remarkable career spanning a total of 49 years and involving three owners and two World Wars.

The stage was now set for the introduction of the most famous

Channel steamer of them all: the one and only *Canterbury*.

The ship was luxury and magnificence personified and was specifically designed to provide the sea-going link of the famed First Class 'Golden Arrow/ Fleche d'Or' luxury train between London Victoria and Paris Gare du Nord. Carrying just 300 Pullman passengers, the *Canterbury* took up service on 15th May 1929 under the command of the Commodore of the Southern Railway fleet, Captain George Blaxland, OBE. It was he who in May 1923 had carried Their Majesties King George V and Queen Mary from Dover to Calais in the *Biarritz* at the start of their State Visit to Italy. Possibly unique in the annals of the British Merchant

*In 1923, the French took over the operation of the **Invicta** and **Empress** which then reverted to white funnels. Here is the **Invicta** at berth 4 on the Admiralty Pier while the **Engadine** slips astern on her arrival from Calais. (John Hendy collection)*

The **Invicta** and **Empress** had their Promenade Decks plated in following the arrival of the Southern Railway's 1925 twins. Second Class accommodation was at the after end. Here is the **Empress** leaving the western exit of Dover Harbour past the World War I block ship markers in April 1927. (AE Glen)

The **Maid of Kent** of 1925 and her earlier sister **Isle of Thanet** were far more enclosed than the previous turbines and marked a new departure in cross-Channel ship design. (John Hendy collection)

Navy, the ship flew the White Ensign of the Admiralty at her foremast and the Royal Standard at the main and was escorted by no fewer than nine destroyers.

The Depression of the early 'thirties soon saw this luxury service trimmed and the Southern could no longer afford to put on an extra ship for the other passengers. During the winter of 1930/31, the *Canterbury* was fitted with Second Class accommodation and in May 1931, the duplication of Dover – Calais services ceased seeing off the old *Riviera* and later her sister the *Engadine* from the local fleet. The former passed to Burns & Laird of Glasgow and as the *Laird's Isle* operated the daylight Ardrossan – Belfast link until 1957 while the latter sailed to the Philippines as the *Corregidor* where she was sunk by the Japanese in 1941.

The new *Canterbury* had not long been in service before Captain Blaxland reported to his Marine Superintendent that a group of Frenchmen had asked to see over his ship during one of her lay-overs in Calais. When permission had been granted, they descended on her and armed with tape measures and notepads, proceeded to inspect the new ship from stem to stern. 'Good,' came the reply, 'it's about time that the French had some new ships!'.

Sure enough, twin vessels of roughly the same dimensions as the flagship of the Southern were ordered from Le Havre ship builders, the first being the *Cote d'Azur* which entered service in April 1931. The almost identical *Cote d'Argent* followed twelve months later and duly replaced the old *Invicta* and *Empress* which were sold for scrap.

The new ships had accommodation for 900 First Class passengers and 500 in the Second Class, the *Cote d'Azur* attaining a trials speed of 23.25 knots against her contract speed of 22.5 knots.

*The wheelhouse of the **Isle of Thanet** as seen on her last day in September 1963. (John Hendy collection)*

*Denny's Leven Yard is seen from the adjacent Dumbarton Rock in May 1926. The **Maid of Orleans** has just undergone conversion to oil burning and has had her Promenade Deck enclosed. The steamer nearest the camera is the renowned Scottish excursion vessel **King George V**. (AE Glen)*

The **Maid of Kent** *in dry dock when new and with the bridge cabs which were so unpopular with the local Masters. Notice too her bow rudder which was unlocked when the vessel was running astern. Today's Health & Safety people would doubtless have had something to say about the trestles used for painting her hull. (AE Glen)*

The 'Golden Arrow' steamer **Canterbury** *(Captain George Blaxland) is seen leaving Dover for Calais early in her career. With just 300 First Class 'Pullman' passengers on board, she epitomised luxury. (John Hendy collection)*

The twins were fairly easy to tell apart by the depth of the black top to their funnels and the fact that the first ship had a narrow blue band below the black funnel top while the second vessel's narrow band was silver. In 1934, SAGA offered the ships to the Southern Railway but national pride intervened and the sale was blocked by the French Ministry of Marine.

CARGO AND CARS

All the old railway companies maintained extensive fleets of cargo carriers for use on their Continental services and the officer promotion process always started in vessels of this type.

The Southern had inherited a fleet of elderly cargo vessels which included the ancient iron-hulled *CW Eborall* of 1882, the *Maidstone* of 1899, the *Canterbury* of 1901, the *Walmer* and *Deal* which were purchased second hand from the London Brighton & South Coast Railway in 1901, the *Folkestone* of 1903 and the *Hythe* of 1905.

Ten new sisters for their cross-Channel services were now ordered from D&W Henderson of Port Glasgow to replace the much older and smaller tonnage. The *Tonbridge* and *Minster* arrived on station in 1924, the *Hythe* and *Whitstable* in 1925, and the *Maidstone* and *Deal* in 1926 and 1928. The other ships in the series, the *Fratton*, *Ringwood* and *Haslemere* were built for the Southampton services while the tenth ship,

The Southern Railway chartered the steam colliers **Abington** *and the elderly* **Dublin** *of 1904 (seen here) during the summer of 1929 in order to compete with Captain Townsend's rival service to Calais. These rare views capture something of the flavour of those days. (John Hendy collection)*

A post-war view of the **Canterbury** *after new engineers' cabins were added to the after end of her Boat Deck. The rather antique looking round-headed windows once illuminated the ship's Palm Court. (John Hendy collection)*

The **Autocarrier** *was the Southern's first purpose-built cross-Channel car ferry. Entering service in 1931, she is seen in the twilight of her career. (FotoFlite)*

SAGA's **Cote d'Azur** *entered service in 1931 but was sadly lost at the evacuation of Dunkirk ten years later. Raised by the Germans, she was mined and sunk in 1945. (John Hendy collection)*

The **Canterbury** *(Captain GD Walker) re-opened the post-war 'Golden Arrow' in April 1946. Calais was then a vastly different place and a temporary Gare Maritime had been constructed. (John Hendy collection)*

The **Canterbury** is seen leaving Southampton in July 1943 complete with heavy davits in preparation for her role as a Landing Ship (Infantry). (John Hendy collection)

A post-war view of the **Biarritz** as a troop carrier berthed alongside at Calais. She was not to return to civilian service and was broken up at Dover in 1950. She was the only local railway ship to serve in two world wars. (National Railway Museum)

originally to be named *Camberley*, was modified on the stocks and became the first purpose-built car carrier on the Channel – the *Autocarrier*.

The conversion became necessary following the introduction of Captain Stuart Townsend's lift on – lift off service for motor cars in July 1928 (see Chapter 6). The Southern countered what they perceived as a threat when in 1929 they chartered the cargo vessels *Dublin* and *Abington* to convey cars from Dover to Calais while placing their new *Whitstable* on a similar service between Folkestone and Boulogne.

The *Autocarrier* carried just 35 crane-loaded cars and 120 passengers and commenced service on the last day of May 1931.

The Southern's next great innovation was the introduction of the cross-Channel train ferry service to Dunkirk in October 1936. With increased cargo levels now being shipped directly to and from the Continent by train, the *Minster* and *Tonbridge* were transferred to the Southampton station.

With the 'Golden Arrow' service as popular as ever, an order was also placed at Denny's for a larger ship to maintain the prestige service. The new *Invicta* (III) was not ready until after the outbreak of war and on 3rd September 1939, Dover Harbour was closed for civilian traffic.

THE SECOND WORLD WAR AND ITS AFTERMATH

Tragically both SAGA vessels were lost during the Second World War. The *Cote d'Argent* was captured by the advancing Germans at Cherbourg during the evacuation of that port and was then converted to a minelayer and later a torpedo target vessel. Renamed the *Ostmark,* she was lost

when the RAF caught up with her in the Kattegat during April 1945. As for the *Cote d'Azur*, she was bombed and sank during the evacuation of Dunkirk in May 1940 but was later raised and as the *Elsass,* used by the Germans as a minelayer and then a helicopter training ship in the Kattegat. In June 1944 she hit a mine and sank near the Danish island of Samso.

Both Dover 'Maids' were also lost during the hostilities. Serving as a hospital ship, the *Maid of Kent* was in the inner docks at Dieppe when on 21st May 1940, bombs were dropped on the quay alongside her. The blast completely destroyed her superstructure, rendering the ship a wreck and killing 17 members of her crew. The *Maid of Orleans* was torpedoed and sank within 30 minutes with a loss of six of her crew when returning from the Normandy Beaches to Newhaven during Operation Neptune on 28th June 1944.

The war in Europe ended in May 1945 and a cargo service between Folkestone and Calais recommenced with the *Hythe* and *Maidstone* that August before in December the *Canterbury* was finally released from duties and sent for refit on the Tyne.

The Dunkirk train ferries had restored a commercial service to Calais as early as February 1946 but it was not until mid-April that a gleaming *Canterbury* returned to re-wing the 'Golden Arrow' and demolished the austerity of the wartime years at a stroke. Six months later, the *Invicta* took up station on the route and service that she was to maintain for another 26 years; the only British Dover Strait passenger steamer to serve upon one route during her entire career.

The new Southampton-based passenger steamer *Falaise* briefly

SAGA's **Cote d'Argent** of 1933 was also captured by the Germans and sunk by the RAF in 1945. (John Hendy collection)

The **Isle of Thanet** served as a hospital ship during the Second World War and is seen alongside at Newhaven. Her sister **Maid of Kent** was lost at Dieppe. (John Hendy collection)

On board the **Invicta**: *a reflection of the comfortable 'Golden Arrow' Pullman cars; the First Class port lounge in October 1946. (John Hendy collection)*

On board the **Invicta**: *the post-war austerity of the First Class port Sun Deck. (John Hendy collection)*

appeared on the 'Golden Arrow' during October 1947 and a new *Maid of Orleans* was ordered primarily for the Folkestone – Boulogne service which had become a seasonal operation.

The Dover – Calais car ferry *Autocarrier* had spent most of the war as a NAAFI ship in Scapa Flow and on her release spent much time in the western Channel based in Southampton. It was appreciated that with the expected increase in cross-Channel traffic after the war, the *Autocarrier*

would be too small and so the Southern Railway converted the 1924-built Southampton – St. Malo overnight steamer *Dinard* for car ferry service. She duly took up a seasonal service from Dover to Boulogne on 1st July 1947.

On New Year's Day 1948, the Nationalisation of Britain's railways saw the creation of the British Transport Commission and the formation of British Railways.

The Southern Railway's **Invicta** *was the first Dover - Calais vessel of over 4,000 gross tons. Her extra deck always gave her a most imposing appearance and she is seen on trials off Dover running full astern, the black balls on her main mast indicating that she is using her bow rudder. (John Hendy collection)*

Flagship of the Southern. Under the command of Captain H.L. Payne, the stately **Invicta** *is seen having just left Dover on her daily run with 'Golden Arrow' passengers to Calais. (Ferry Publications Library)*

CHAPTER THREE

SNCF & BR: 'THE BIG FLEET' AND SEALINK

We have seen how French operators SAGA (owned by Rothchild's Bank) lost both of their passenger steamers – the *Cote d'Azur* and *Cote d'Argent* - during the Second World War. The French National Railways (Societe Nationale des Chemins de Fer Francais - SNCF) replaced them with the Calais – Folkestone passenger vessel *Cote d'Azur* (II) in 1950 followed by the Danish-built diesel-powered train ferry *Saint-Germain* for the Dunkirk – Dover link in 1951. Had the two pre-war steamers survived hostilities then the subsequent history of the Calais – Dover route would have doubtless been quite different. It is worthwhile noting that both pairs of pre-war steamers were never in service together. While one ship maintained the morning mail service, the other was on stand-by/ refit – a luxury which no operator could afford today. The railways of France were nationalised in 1938.

By the mid-fifties, British Railways had firmly established their new car ferry service on the Dover – Boulogne link using the converted passenger steamer *Dinard* (70 cars) and the new *Lord Warden* (120 cars) which in 1952 became the Dover Strait's first purpose-built drive on – drive off car ferry.

The Dover – Calais passage was operated by Townsend Bros. Car Ferries, with their converted frigate *Halladale* (55 cars). Established in 1928, the seasonal service had seen slow but steady growth since her replacement of the ancient *Forde* in 1950 (see Chapter 6).

It was against this background that SNCF ordered its first car ferry

*The former Southampton-based **Normannia** was converted from a passenger steamer to a car ferry and entered service at Dover in April 1964. (AG Jones)*

from the Rouen yard of Societe des Chantiers Reunis Loire Normandie. The ship was launched on 7th March 1958 and was due in service on 30th May.

The *Compiegne* continued the tradition of naming Calais-based vessels with 'C' and proved to be a most innovative ship boasting a number of features which, although the norm these days, were ground breaking in 1958. Most importantly, the ship was built with controllable pitch

*The passenger steamer **St Patrick** was built for the Great Western Railway in 1948 and came to the Dover Strait in December 1964. (AG Jones)*

*The car ferry **Maid of Kent** was the third local ship to carry that famous name. She was switched to the Weymouth station in 1974 and became British Rail's last operational steamship. (AG Jones)*

*The car ferry **Lord Warden** is seen in February 1969 when she was deputising on the 'Golden Arrow' route. (AG Jones)*

The **Dover** of 1965 was British Rail's last turbine steamer to be built for Dover Strait services and is seen leaving Boulogne. In 1977 she was converted to drive-through operations and renamed **Earl Siward**. (AG Jones)

SNCF's **Compiegne** was the first French car ferry and entered service in 1958 introducing many new design concepts. At the time of writing, this trend-setting ferry is still afloat. (AG Jones)

The **Chantilly** *off service and alongside at the Gare Maritime in April 1969. (AG Jones)*

Leaving Calais in April 1969, the **Invicta** *passes the* **Chantilly** *and leaves the* **Compiegne** *and* **Normannia** *astern in the port's twin linkspans. (AG Jones)*

*Truly the end of an era; The one and only **Canterbury** (Captain W Walters) arriving off Dover for lay-up pending sale in September 1964. (John Hendy)*

*At the end of her first season in service, at Easter 1966 the **Dover** is escorted into the Wellington Dock by the DHB tug **Diligent**. (John Hendy)*

propellers which the Captain operated directly from the bridge rather than via the Chief Engineer in the Engine Room. She was also built of all-welded construction which certainly sped up the overall building process and allowed for a degree of prefabrication. The ship also introduced a stern docking bridge which was to be used when she was berthing stern first at Dover and Calais. It was claimed that she was the model for the future and she carried 164 cars on three levels with a certificate for 1,000 one-class passengers. The ship was extensively furnished in modern materials designed to give the impression of light and space, she had a Dining Room for 132 and was driven by two V16 Pielstick supercharged diesels each of 4,500 hp and revving at 345 rpm.

The *Compiegne's* stern door had a headroom of 12 ft 6 ins thereby allowing coaches or lorries to be carried in addition to cars and the main vehicle deck led to two other decks at the forward end each with a 7 ft 4.5 ins headroom. The car decks were protected by a sturdy MacGregor/ Mege Jacknife door.

Delays at the shipyard saw the Dunkirk train ferry *Saint-Germain* brought in to operate the new car ferry service until 18th July when Captain J. Lacoste introduced the *Compiegne* into the schedules which required her to operate three round trips each day.

Original plans were for the new ship to assist the British Railways car ferries on the Dover – Boulogne route during the winter months when there was simply not enough traffic to justify the operation of a Calais car ferry.

To celebrate the introduction of the first French car ferry, the mayor and 150 guests from the town of Compiegne crossed in the ship at the end of September. By the end of the season the ship had carried 114,586 passengers and had proved such a success that it was reported that SNCF were considering a second such car ferry.

The year 1958 saw two million passengers pass through Dover for the first time although the bulk of the traffic was still via the train connected services at the Admiralty Pier and it was noted that some 20,000 fewer people travelled by First Class than in the previous twelve months.

At the end of October 1959, the *Compiegne* saw passenger service on the Calais- Folkestone service in place of the *Cote d'Azur* and this was to become a regular feature over the next few seasons. In February 1960, she appeared on the Dover – Boulogne link in place of the *Lord Warden* which was off service for repairs and the new BR car ferry *Maid of Kent* which was on her first overhaul.

The old order changed when on 15th September 1963, the veteran steamer *Isle of Thanet* was withdrawn from service after completing her

final crossing on the Folkestone – Boulogne route. She passed for scrap at Blyth in the following June and then on 27th September 1964, the *Canterbury* also finished service at the close of the Folkestone – Boulogne season. She too steamed to Dover's Wellington Dock to await her fate before departure to Antwerp for breaking in July 1965.

Replacements arrived firstly in the form of the 1952-built *Normannia*. The Southampton passenger steamer had closed the overnight Le Havre route in December 1963 after which she was immediately sent to the Tyne for conversion to a car ferry for the Dover – Boulogne link. With the withdrawn *Isle of Thanet's* crew on board, she took up sailings on 21st April 1964. The second 'new' ship was the passenger steamer *St. Patrick* of 1948 which was transferred to the Dover Strait in December 1964 initially operating on Dover – Calais reliefs before settling down on the Folkestone – Boulogne seasonal service in 1965.

The long-awaited second SNCF car ferry was launched by Dubigeon Normandie SA at Nantes on 9th November 1965 and named *Chantilly*. As with the *Compiegne* eight years earlier, she boasted a number of new features: a nursery for mothers and children, an escalator from her car decks to the passenger areas and closed-circuit television showing films in some of the lounges. Her 12-cylinder engines (each developing 4,750 hp at 370 rpm) provided the same power as the earlier ship's 16-cylinder engines and her capacity was for 1,200 passengers and 210 cars.

After completing a press trip on 17th June 1966 when she called at Dover, Newhaven and Boulogne, she operated her maiden voyage between Calais and Dover on 21st June relieving her hard-worked sister

*SNCF's second car ferry was the attractive-looking **Chantilly** which is seen arriving at Dover from Calais when new in July 1966. (John Hendy)*

*A happy occasion with the newly arrived **Vortigern** dressed overall on the Admiralty Pier's berth 3. The **Invicta** lies astern while ALA's Dunkirk ferry **Twickenham Ferry** sits in the train ferry dock. (John Hendy collection)*

with which to name their fleet. The traditional names were consigned to history and in 1980, 'Saint' names were adopted.

1970 AND A CHANGE OF EMPHASIS

Until 1970, British Rail ships had maintained the Dover – Boulogne car ferry service while SNCF had competed with Townsend Car Ferries for traffic on the Dover – Calais route. However, this state of affairs was to change dramatically over the next few years and culminated in the complete withdrawal of the Boulogne service while every effort was forthcoming to promote Dover to Calais as the premier link.

The year 1970 marked very much a turning point and witnessed the beginnings of the decline in traffic to Boulogne at the expense of Calais. Between mid-July and mid-September some 64 weekly round sailings were operated to Calais instead of the 38 in 1969. During the same period, Boulogne had its sailings cut from 78 to 66.

The reason for this policy change lay primarily at the door of the British Rail hovercraft division Hoverspeed, which had introduced the first SRN 4 craft *The Princess Margaret* onto the Dover – Boulogne crossing in August 1968. A sister craft *The Princess Anne* followed and during the next ten years this competition was to rule the minds and planning of those who operated the service. The whole hovercraft concept was so powerful that the ferry division suffered at a time when their competitor Townsend Car Ferries was investing heavily in new tonnage and in their new route to Zeebrugge in Belgium. Instead of competing with Townsend, British Rail through their ship and hovercraft

for a week before commencing her own advertised sailings. The occasion was somewhat marred when on 2nd July, the *Chantilly* managed to wrap a wire hawser around one of her screws and missed two sailings while it was being removed.

The *Chantilly's* call at Newhaven during her press trip pointed to occasional use on the Dieppe service on which her half sisters *Villandry* and *Valencay* (of 1965) operated with BR's steamer *Falaise*. She first saw service on the longer route over Easter 1967 but in mid-September that year she saw an unusual charter to a Roman Catholic organisation when the Papal flag was flown at her masthead. Then during November, she enjoyed a week's charter to Townsend Car Ferries who badly required extra capacity following the grounding of their freighter *Autocarrier*.

Entering service between Dover and Boulogne on 31st July 1969 came the Tyne-built multi-purpose vessel *Vortigern*, the first diesel-powered cross-Channel vessel in the local railway fleet. She was also the first with variable-pitched propellers making her a revolutionary ship as far as her local managers and crews were concerned. The ship was to operate as a car ferry during the summer months and then switch to the Dover – Dunkirk train ferry route in the winter and as such was the most versatile of all the railway-owned ships. However, the sudden surge in roll on – roll off traffic over the next few years was to change this plan and the small, low-headroomed car ferries driven by increasingly expensive heavy fuel oil were to find that this was now an age in which they did not belong.

In choosing the name *Vortigern* for their new ship, the British Railways Board introduced a ten-year period of characters from the 'Dark Ages'

*SNCF's **Compiegne** arriving at Dover Eastern Docks in August 1967. (John Hendy)*

In the worst gales of the season, under the command of Captain Elgar Blaxland, the **Invicta** *sets off to Calais for the final time on 8th August 1972. (AG Jones)*

subsidiaries, competed with themselves. The downgrading of the Dover – Boulogne car ferry service allowed the hovercraft service a free reign while the ferries of SNCF and BR took on Townsend on the shorter crossing.

The first attempt at a joint marketing policy between the combined French and British fleets had been made in 1965 when they had created 'The Big Fleet'. However, at a press conference in November 1969, it was announced that the British Rail Shipping & International Services Division had adopted a new brand name: Sealink.

The *Dover* took up the Dover – Calais service in place of the Chantilly in January 1970 when the French car ferry was used for passenger-only sailings. The *Maid of Kent* then took over the schedules until the return of the *Chantilly* in April.

For the summer season, the 1952-built *Lord Warden* transferred to Dover – Calais and the clear-cut distinction between SNCF at Calais and BR at Boulogne was ended. The *Compiegne* was even used on a Dover – Boulogne service between her usual Calais – Dover runs.

However, the *Lord Warden's* summer stint was terminated on 2nd August when running astern into Calais, she was in collision with the quayside which resulted in damage to her starboard quarter. With a spare screw and propeller shaft on board, she subsequently sailed to Harland & Wolff's dry dock in the Royal Albert Dock, London and with no spare ships available her sailings were cancelled.

The year 1970 also saw SNCF's *Chantilly* involved in three special passenger sailings from Dieppe and up the River Seine to Rouen, sailing out one day and back the next. These cruises proved to be very popular

The **Earl Leofric** (*ex* **Holyhead Ferry I**) *departing Calais for Dover while the* **Horsa** *loads for Folkestone in May 1980. (John Hendy)*

During the 1973 season, the **Normannia** *ran for SNCF with a French crew and registered in Calais. The Belgian ferry* **Prins Philippe** *towers over her. (John Hendy)*

The second **Maid of Orleans** *alongside at Calais. She closed the 'Golden Arrow' service in September 1972 but thereafter operated on the seasonal train-connected services until her withdrawal three years later. (AG Jones)*

and were repeated during the following seasons.

The year 1971 saw the *Lord Warden* back on the peak-season Calais car ferry service following a period of operation during April with the *Maid of Kent*.

The end of the season marked the retirement of the passenger steamer *St. Patrick*. After having been painted in the new British Rail livery, she had arrived at Dover in December 1964 to take up relief sailings to Calais. The ship had been built at Cammell Laird, Birkenhead in 1948 and during her previous career had been mainly associated with the Weymouth – Channel Islands service. Now surplus to requirements, she was to spend her last seasons on the seasonal Folkestone – Boulogne link (in place of the withdrawn *Isle of Thanet* and *Canterbury*) but frequently

spent winter spells on the Dover – Calais service covering Agents' Specials or the 'Golden Arrow' when the *Invicta* or *Maid of Orleans* were not available.

An unusual visitor to the Dover – Calais route during early October 1971 was the Newhaven – Dieppe car ferry *Falaise* which worked the service vice the *Maid of Kent* for ten days.

With the *Invicta* briefly off service during November, the *Chantilly* was called in to incorporate her schedules and in February 1972, the turbine steamer retired to the Wellington Dock when the *Lord Warden* deputised on the most famous service of all.

Imports of Chrysler cars from Dieppe to Newhaven saw the *Chantilly* on that service for four days during early February while a month later

A most unusual visitor to Dover; the former Heysham-based steamer **Duke of Rothesay** *was briefly used on the Dover - Calais passenger service in June-July 1974 while the* **Maid of Orleans** *was away operating to the Channel Islands. (AG Jones)*

The **Vortigern** *at sea following the conversion of her after garage to a lounge and the rearrangement of her lifeboats in 1978. (FotoFlite)*

the *Compiegne* was sent to assist in this trade. She made just two trips as she was found not to be sufficiently manoeuvrable for the small French port.

With both the *Maid of Kent* and the *Chantilly* engaged on passenger-only sailings during April 1972, the smaller *Lord Warden* and *Normannia* took turns on the Dover – Calais car ferry service through until June. Meanwhile, the *Compiegne* was used again on the Calais – Folkestone link at the end of April after the regular steamer *Cote d'Azur* had suffered a break down.

The major event of 1972 was the arrival of the Brest-built *Hengist* and *Horsa* and the opening of Folkestone as a car ferry port on 1st July. Unfortunately the *Hengist* failed with fuel-pump problems on the opening

day and the *Vortigern* was switched to cover. So many passengers were on offer at Folkestone on 4th July that the *Invicta* was switched from Dover to deputise while the *Vortigern* stood-in on the Dover – Calais 'Golden Arrow' service.

The summer of 1972 saw the Dover – Calais car ferry service maintained by the *Compiegne* and *Chantilly* working with British Rail's *Dover*. The *Hengist's* sister ship *Horsa* arrived on 2nd August and both new ships carried the trading name 'Sealink' on their hulls while the rest of the fleet followed in 1973.

Tuesday 8th August witnessed the end of an era with the final day of the 'Golden Arrow' steamer *Invicta* and on the following day the *Maid of Orleans*, displaced from Folkestone by the new car ferries, took over her

The **Holyhead Ferry I** *having problems berthing in September 1974. She was sent for conversion to drive-through operations in 1976 and re-emerged as the* **Earl Leofric***. (John Hendy)*

The **Maid of Orleans** *(Captain G Sutcliffe) coming astern into Dover during her penultimate season. Built in 1949 for the summer Folkestone - Boulogne link, she regularly deputised on the winter 'Golden Arrow' service. (John Hendy)*

The **Chartres** *entered service in 1974 as a multi-purpose passenger, car, train ferry and as such her hull dimensions were almost identical to those of the* **Vortigern** *and ALA's* **Saint Eloi***. (FotoFlite)*

schedule. This famous service, started by the *Canterbury* in May 1929 finally ended on the final day of September 1972. At the commencement of the winter timetable the following day, the 'Golden Arrow' sailings were embraced by the *Hengist* and *Horsa's* schedules. They were one-class ships and so the famous train was terminated. The new rosters no longer required a passenger vessel on the Folkestone – Calais route and so the *Cote d'Azur* was retired on the same day. Thus on 1st October 1972, car ferries reigned supreme on the Dover Strait and it was no longer possible to cross the Channel in a passenger-only ship.

Before the end of the year, the Southampton-registered *Normannia* was relieving on the Dover – Calais route while the *Dover* was at Newhaven deputising for the two French car ferries on the Dieppe link. Newhaven's British car ferry, the converted *Falaise*, made a second brief appearance as a relief ferry on the Calais route at the close of September.

With a new ship on order for the 1974 season, SNCF now purchased the *Normannia* for 1973 and operated her with a French crew, under the French tricolour and re-registered her in Calais.

The *Dover's* half sister, Holyhead's *Holyhead Ferry I*, appeared at Dover during the first three months of 1973 while on return from her refit, the *Dover* replaced the *Normannia* which began her season under the French flag with a special sailing from St. Malo to Jersey on 28th April.

The old pattern of Calais sailings from Dover every three hours was in operation during the 1973 summer season with three vessels running to both Calais and Boulogne while in addition, the passenger steamer *Maid of Orleans* operated Dover – Calais train-connected services.

The new SNCF multi-purpose vessel *Chartres* was launched at Dubigeon-Normandie at Nantes on 12th September allowing the *Normannia* to return to the Red Ensign on 23rd October. The *Chartres* entered service in a train ferry mode, crossing from Dunkirk to Dover on 25th February 1974 while later that year, Dover bade farewell to the *Maid of Kent* which was transferred to Weymouth for the seasonal Cherbourg link. In this role she lasted until the end of September 1981 when she became Sealink's final operational steamship.

The summer operation of the passenger ship *Maid of Orleans* on the Dover – Calais link continued as it had done in 1973 but on 28th June she was switched to the Weymouth – Channel Islands route to cover for the *Sarnia* for ten days. During this period, Sealink transferred the stately *Duke of Rothesay* to run the traditional Dover – Calais passenger sailings on the old 'Golden Arrow' timings. She had been built for the overnight Heysham – Belfast passenger link in 1956 but had been converted to a car ferry in May 1967 at which time she was switched to the Fishguard – Rosslare service across St. George's Channel.

The car ferry *Dover* spent the 1974 season operating from Holyhead to Dun Laoghaire while the *Holyhead Ferry I* (with her smaller car capacity – 160 against 205) came round to the Dover – Calais service in company with the *Compiegne* and *Chantilly*.

The *Normannia* had the misfortune to sink in Dover Harbour on 25th July. While berthing at the completion of a day's sailings, she hit the remains of one of the old paddle steamer berths at the end of the Admiralty Pier Extension. Both Dover Harbour Board tugs were quickly on the scene and towed her to the Tidal Basin for beaching and patching. The ship was never quite the same again having had her engines and electrics flooded with sea water and on completion of her repairs at Middlesbrough, she sailed to Weymouth to deputise for the failed *Falaise*.

The year 1975 started with the *Chartres* deputising at Dieppe and the switch, during March, of the *Dover* and the *Holyhead Ferry I*, the latter working to both Calais and Boulogne. During the summer season the visitor was used on the Boulogne service while the *Vortigern* switched to work Calais with the French ships.

On 27th September 1975, the *Maid of Orleans* completed her final sailing between Dover and Calais in quite the worst weather of the season which deprived her of an anticipated attempt to better her record run of 58 minutes pier to pier.

Replacing her for the following season was the passenger steamer *Caesarea* which completed her final voyage between Jersey and Weymouth on 6th October.

November 1975 saw the *Chartres* at Newhaven while SNCF sent the Dieppe-based ferry *Valencay* to Calais at the end of the month to replace the *Compiegne* on the Folkestone and Dover links.

The first day of 1976 saw Newhaven's *Senlac* (sister ship to the *Hengist* and *Horsa*) on the Dover and Folkestone to Boulogne routes before briefly appearing on services from the English ports to Calais.

CONVERSIONS FOR FREIGHT TRAFFIC

The dramatic increase in roll on – roll off freight traffic throughout the early seventies, found much of the Sealink fleet struggling to cope. It had for long been the policy of the British Railways Board to put all such traffic on the Dover – Dunkirk train ferries using their vehicle ferries to carry mainly tourist cars and passengers. With Townsend leading the way at Dover and quick to exploit the transport revolution which was unfolding, both BR and SNCF required a major reassessment of their policy. Both concerns were extremely reluctant to build new tonnage as not only were costs and delays to be considered but also the continuing question of whether a Channel Tunnel would be built. Conversions of existing tonnage would therefore be quicker and cheaper.

As early as December 1969, the *Compiegne* had been sent to Le Havre for a two-month conversion in order to have her stern raised in order to

accommodate extra freight at her after end. However, the first vessel to be properly dealt with was the *Chantilly* which left service for her conversion to drive-through operations between December 1975 and January 1976. The *Holyhead Ferry I* was sent to Swan Hunter on the Tyne for similar treatment costing £1.85 million. During this period of surgery, she lost her passenger cabins thereby giving her vehicle capacity similar to that of her close sister, the *Dover*. The ship was changed so much that Sealink decided to rename her *Earl Leofric*. Leofric was the 11th century Earl of Mercia, colleague of King Canute and was the husband of the infamous Lady Godiva.

The early part of 1976 saw both the *Normannia* and *Lord Warden* on the Dover – Calais service while the passenger steamer *Caesarea* arrived at Dover from Weymouth on 3rd February.

Unfortunately, the conversion of the *Holyhead Ferry I/ Earl Leofric* took far longer than anticipated and so Sealink were forced to charter the spare Belgian car ferry *Artevelde* (of 1958) between 30th June and 7th September. The ship worked the *Earl Leofric's* intended timetable but was quite unable to accommodate all the freight vehicles on offer. The 'Leofric' finally arrived from on Tyne on 23rd September starting three days late on the first day of the winter timetable. With a reduced passenger certificate for just 725 and an extra four lifeboats, the steamer celebrated her homecoming on a passage from Boulogne during the worst gales of the year on 14th October when she crossed in 20 hours.

The new Port Rapide at Dunkirk West opened for traffic on 5th July 1976 when, apart from the train ferry service, Sealink hoped to attract freight operators. An afternoon sailing from Dover Eastern Docks using the *Normannia* was initially tried but she was far too small and the *Compiegne* took over from her at the end of November.

The *Dover's* conversion to drive-through took place at the Danish port of Aalborg where she arrived during late September. A fixed price of £1.96 million was quoted against the best British quote of £3.01 million

The former Weymouth - Channel Islands steamer **Caesarea** *was switched to the Dover Strait between 1976 - 1980 before her sale to Hong Kong owners. (AG Jones)*

The **Earl Siward** (ex **Dover**) *is unusually seen with her starboard side alongside in the Wellington Dock. In her twin incarnations, she enjoyed a brief 16-year career before being sold to Cyprus for further service.* (AG Jones)

with completion for autumn 1977. The ship was renamed *Earl Siward* after the 11th century Dane who became Earl of Northumbria and made his name for an invasion of Scotland where he defeated Macbeth. The *Earl Siward* arrived back at Dover on 1st July 1977 six weeks late due to the late delivery of equipment from Britain.

Earlier in the year the *Earl Leofric* had been working the Dunkirk West and Ostend services before joining her converted sister on the Dover - Calais route for the summer. The twin conversions proved to be very much stop-gap measures before purpose-built tonnage was ordered for the 1980 season.

The *Compiegne* was again called to Dieppe during early September 1977 after the *Valencay* had damaged herself when the *Normannia* was brought in to take her Dover – Calais timings until the end of the summer timetable. It was almost the end of the road for the diminutive car ferry but after finishing at Dover on 20th January 1978, Weymouth had further need of her during the first half of the New Year. It was then a period of lay-up at Newhaven before sailing for scrap in Spain on 29th November.

Early in 1978, it was announced that two new ships were to be ordered for the Dover – Calais route for entry into service during 1980. They would be the largest railway-owned vessels yet for the historic route and would boast drive-through facilities on two decks. Each was to cost £28 million and would carry 1,000 passengers and 300 cars or 60 lorries.

The *Lord Warden* returned from the Irish Sea to do a period of relief during the early part of 1978 at which time the *Earl Leofric* was deputising on Newhaven – Dieppe while during the height of the summer, the French veteran *Compiegne* was scheduled to run just two daily round trips between Boulogne and Dover. With the *Lord Warden* based at Fishguard during the summer of 1978, this was to be the first summer since 1888 that the port of Dover failed to have at least one ship

in operation that was built by the famous Denny of Dumbarton yard. The 'Warden' did, however, return to Dover for a final time in late November – early October to stand in for the *Compiegne*. After one final season on the Irish Sea, she was sold to Saudi Arabian buyers and as the *Al Zaher* ended her days as scrap at Gadani Beach in Pakistan.

SEALINK UK LTD

On the first day of 1979, a new British Rail shipping subsidiary was born superseding the Shipping and International Services Division. Sealink UK Ltd was to steer the company into its eventual privatisation five years later.

That summer the *Compiegne* and *Chantilly* were maintaining the Dover – Boulogne link while the Calais service was left in the hands of the *Earl Leofric, Earl Siward* and *Chartres*. In response to Sealink UK's pending introduction of new tonnage, SNCF now ordered their own new ship after which time it was expected that the *Chartres* would find full time occupation as a train ferry replacing the elderly *Saint-Germain*.

On 4th December 1979, Lady Parker (wife of British Rail Chairman, Sir Peter Parker) named the first of the new BR ships in gale force winds at Harland & Wolff's Belfast yard. The weather was so bad that the *St Anselm* was not actually launched until the strong winds had abated on the following day. The ship was named after an Archbishop of Canterbury who had died in 1105 and represented the new Sealink policy of naming ships after 'Saints' rather than characters from the Dark Ages.

There were also gale force winds blowing across Belfast when the second of the ships was named on 18th March 1980 by a presenter on the BBC children's programme 'Blue Peter', Miss Tina Heath. It was not until two days later that the actual launch took place and there cannot be many instances where sister ships have both been subjected to delays of this nature. However, during the following months, construction of the

The St Anselm (Commodore John Arthur) became the Flagship of the British Rail (Sealink) fleet and both she and her sister were the most manoeuvrable ferries in the Dover Strait. (John Hendy)

twins was to fall badly behind.

There was a degree of discussion concerning the name of the second ship with both 'St Augustine' and 'St Dunstan' being considered. These were both 'local' names and had much to recommend them but eventually, the BRB opted for the safe name of *St Christopher* – the patron saint of travellers.

It soon became very obvious that the new ships would not be ready in time for the 1980 season and Sealink UK's Chairman, Michael Bosworth, complained of the late delivery. For the builders, Sir Brian Morton said that there were times when building a ship seemed more difficult than sending a man to the moon.

Sealink's competitors Townsend Thoresen had gone to West Germany for their three new ships for the Dover – Calais service and they were all delivered according to schedule. Due to the Government constraints on the nationalised Sealink UK, Belfast was given the contract to build four new ships – one for Stranraer, two for Dover and the fourth for Fishguard (later Holyhead) and all were delivered late. Sealink were, needless to say, upset. The *St Anselm* was due in service at 11.30 on 1st July while the *St Christopher* was to be ready for the 01.00 on 28th September. It was not until the morning of 24th October that the first ship finally arrived in her home port.

The *St Anselm* had previously left Belfast at midday on 22nd October and had not been sailing south for very long before both radars failed. Fortunately there were five navigating officers on the bridge and after the fault had been rectified, the ship ran into a force 8-9 gale with long Atlantic swells in St. George's Channel. Rounding Land's End, the gales eased and final trials were carried out in the lee of Falmouth, time even

being found to circumnavigate the Eddystone lighthouse. As the 'Anselm' came up the English Channel, the weather improved and everything was quite perfect when Dover's new ship entered harbour for the first time.

Sealink UK's Senior Master, Captain John Arthur had previously been promoted to Fleet Commodore and said that his prayers had been answered when the sun shone on his new command as she sailed into Dover Bay at the end of her delivery voyage.

Ramp trials and the taking on of stores was the first job but on Sunday 26th October, the ship crossed to Calais for the first time for ramp tests there. Gales had unfortunately returned as the ship left Dover at 05.45 to test the inner linkspans (numbers 3 and 4) adjacent to the Gare Maritime. Departing from Calais at 11.00, the ship was off Dover 90 minutes later, entering through the eastern entrance before sailing across the harbour to berth on the Admiralty Pier.

The *St Anselm*'s maiden voyage was the 07.00 to Calais on Monday 27th October in place of the *Earl Leofric* which had completed her final scheduled sailing with the 05.15 from Calais that morning. After de-storing, the turbine steamer was sent to Newhaven to lay-up but on 2nd November, the *Earl Siward* stripped some turbine blades and the 'Leofric' was brought back a week later. The 'Siward' finally re-entered service on 11th December but the 'Leofric' lingered for four more days after the new ship went off service for minor repairs. On her return on the 11.30 on 17th December, the 'Leofric' de-stored for the second time and retired to Newhaven. She left for scrapping in northern Spain on 30th May 1981.

With the end of the summer season 1980 came the final sailings of the passenger steamer *Caesarea* which in her brief five-year association with the Dover Strait, had earned many friends among her passengers and

*The **St Anselm** on passage between Dover-Calais. (FotoFlite)*

*The final steamship to operate from Dover was the much-travelled **Caledonian Princess** which is seen leaving for Boulogne during her 1981 season. (AG Jones)*

crew alike. A series of 'Farewell' cruises were organised before she crossed for the final time between Folkestone and Boulogne on 4th October. By the end of the year she was on her way to Hong Kong owners.

Another ship to complete her final advertised sailings in 1980 was the *Compiegne* with the 22.30 from Dover to Boulogne on 27th September after which she sailed for lay-up in the inner harbour at Calais. She was replaced in the SNCF fleet by the third-named *Cote d'Azur* which was launched in heavy rain at Le Havre on 22nd December.

As will have been seen, at this period of the route's history the joint fleets of Sealink UK and SNCF possessed such a large and varied fleet which, in case of emergency, enabled tonnage to be switched around from route to route with comparative ease. This frequently saw some strange combinations of vessels in operation with each other but the important factor was to maintain the service, especially as many of the sailings connected with international trains. How different things are today with no spare tonnage available and the inevitable cancellations if a ship is out of service.

When during mid-January 1981 the *Vortigern* was withdrawn from the Dover – Calais route following an engine room fire, the *Earl Siward* was called in to cover. However, two days later the steamer also went off service with urgent boiler problems and so the *Compiegne* was reactivated and put back into service until 26th February. During this time she was placed back on the route for which she was built making a very unbalanced partnership with the *St Anselm* and the *Chartres*. The *Earl Siward* had a very difficult final spell of operation being off for 'urgent repairs' at the end of February followed by an offshore wire around one of her screws during the following week. The 'Siward' ended her 16-year association with the Dover Strait at the conclusion of her 11.50 sailing from Calais to Folkestone on 14th April.

As the new *St Christopher* was nearing completion in Belfast, it became increasingly certain that Sealink's long-awaited second ship for Dover would be further delayed. She was desperately required to relieve the Fishguard-based ferry *Stena Normandica* and Dover was desperately disappointed that they would in effect receive the ship second hand. The ship finally left Harland & Wolff on 14th March and sailed directly to Rosslare (Co. Wexford) for ramp tests.

At this time, the Holyhead ferry *St. Columba* broke down, yet again, and so the new ship sailed up the Irish coast to Dun Laoghaire (Co. Dublin) and thence to Holyhead where she arrived at midnight on 15th March. After moving to the repair berth at 07.00 the next morning, she took the afternoon sailing from Holyhead on 17th March and then sailed to Fishguard taking up service with the 14.45 two days later. Once the port's own vessel had arrived back from repairs on 12th April, the *St Christopher* left for Dover two hours later, arriving there at 14.00 on the following day. She completed her third maiden voyage within a month when she operated the 08.15 from Dover to Calais on 15th April allowing

*SNCF's **Cote d'Azur** entered service in late 1981 becoming the French contribution to Sealink's 'Flagship Service'. (John Hendy collection)*

The **St Christopher** *arrives at the Eastern Docks from Calais in April 1983. (Miles Cowsill)*

The **St Anselm** *and* **Cote d'Azur**. *(FotoFlite)*

*The arrival of the **Champs Elysees** at Calais in September 1984. Her port of registry indicated that she was not a Calais ship as SNCF planned that she should restart the Boulogne - Dover service. (Miles Cowsill)*

the relieving *Chantilly* to stand down.

Townsend Thoresen had marketed their Dover – Calais crossing as 'Blue Riband Service' after their record-breaking trio of 'Spirit' class ferries. In response, Sealink opted for 'Flagship Service' which was initially operated by the two new 'Saints' and SNCF's *Chartres*. However, at the end of May when the latter vessel went off for repairs, she was replaced by the *Chantilly* while out of retirement for ten days on the Boulogne route to replace her came the *Compiegne*.

Another historic milestone was passed at the end of the 1981 season when Dover's very last turbine steamer, the much-travelled *Caledonian Princess* ended service. She had started her final season at the end of May running a round trip to Calais and a round trip to Boulogne every afternoon. The twenty-year-old vessel, Denny's last railway steamer, had a disappointing season suddenly being called back to maintain the Channel Islands links. In her place Sealink chartered the spare Townsend Thoresen ferry *Free Enterprise III* which commenced service on 25th June for 15 days. At the end of the season on 26th September, the steamer crossed for the final time in the worst gales of the season. Thereafter it was to Newhaven before sale and a new life as the floating nightclub, *Tuxedo Princess*, on the River Tyne at Gateshead. In September 2008, the ship was towed to Turkey for demolition.

Two more disposals occurred during 1981: the *Earl Siward* sailed from Newhaven to Cyprus as the *Sol Express* on 25th November, her new owners inviting former engineers to join them. Five years later, she returned to the UK serving as a nightclub firstly on the River Tyne and then the River Tees as the *Tuxedo Royale*. The former *Dover* is presently (2009) laid up in Hartlepool.

SNCF's first car ferry, the *Compiegne* became the *Ionian Glory*, sailing from Calais on 24th October. It was calculated that the premier French car ferry had completed 22,712 crossings of the Channel during her 23-year career; she had indeed served her owners well. In June 1982, the

Ionian Glory duly took up service linking Brindisi and Patras while in the following December she assisted with the evacuation of Palestinians from Beirut. In 1988 she was chartered to Seven Island Lines and used again in the Adriatic before sale to the Cypriot-owned Vergina Lines in 1989 after which she was named *Queen Vergina*. A further sale in 1990 saw her pass to Maltese owners when she was named *Freedom 1*, spending long periods laid up in Elefsis in Greece. In 1990-91 she was used as an accommodation vessel in Malmo (Sweden) when once again she passed through the Dover Strait before her return to lay up. After her owners had been declared bankrupt, she was sold firstly to Swedish and then Saudi Arabian owners and was renamed *Katerina* for use as a pilgrim ship in the Red Sea. In 1995 she was sold again, renamed *Al Amira* and laid up in Alexandria, Egypt. Whilst there, a further name, *Al Ameerah* was bestowed upon her.

NEW SHIPS FOR SNCF

SNCF's contribution to the 'Flagship Service' had been expected to join the Calais – Dover route on 16th August but did not finally arrive in her home port until 27th September. The *Cote d'Azur* undertook trials at both Dover and Folkestone two days later and entered service with the 07.15 from Calais on 7th October allowing the *St Anselm* to sail to Dunkirk for a mini-refit.

It had been planned to Christen the ship at Calais on 27th October but the crews chose that period to commence a 72-hour strike and so the ceremony was postponed until 2nd December. At this time she was showing the flag in the Pool of London tying up alongside HMS *Belfast* on the previous day after an 8 hour 30 minute crossing from Calais. Her visit coincided with the World Travel Market at Olympia and her vehicle decks were converted into showrooms publicising a whole range of French goods. At the same time it was announced that her passenger certificate would be extended from 1,400 to 1,600 before she finally left

London at 17.00 on 6th December and returning to service two days later.

During spring 1982, SNCF ordered a sister ship for the *Cote d'Azur* which was due to enter service two years later. The order went to Dubigeon Normandie at Nantes and a degree of political wrangling surrounded her. It appears that the maritime wing of SNCF, the Armement Naval, were not particularly anxious to receive another large ship but the Mayor of neighbouring Boulogne also headed the Marine Ministry and was anxious to improve the lot of the city which he represented. A new double-deck, double-width linkspan was ordered and the new ship would have use of it.

Senior Sealink officials at Dover were horrified as Dover – Boulogne had ceased to play any significant role in their scheme of things and placing the new ship on the route would simply serve to weaken their position on the Calais link. The Calais Chamber of Commerce hoped that she would be called 'Cote d'Opale' but instead she was named *Champs Elysees* (Fields of Heaven) after the famous and busy thoroughfare in the centre of Paris. To emphasise the fact that she was not a Calais ship, her port of registry was Nantes.

It was planned that the *Champs Elysees* would replace the *Chantilly* on 3rd June 1984 and that she would boast a massive passenger certificate for 1,800 people.

With both the *St Anselm* and *St Christopher* having capacity for just 1,000 and remembering that when first envisaged, they were not intended to carry many more than 600 people (Sealink management then being certain that by the time they entered service, hovercraft would be taking the bulk of Channel passengers), work was set in hand to increase this by 200. During 1982, the British sisters had their bridge decks aft of their twin funnels opened up and with clear, plastic sheeting fitted across the new railings, the deck proved to be very popular providing an excellent viewing platform protected from the wind. Plans were in hand

to further increase their passenger capacity to 1,400 by extending the accommodation right aft and fitting a self-service duty-free area.

On 5th August 1982 the two SNCF vehicle ferries *Cote d'Azur* (on the 02.00 to Dover) and *Chantilly* (on the 03.45 to Calais) collided off the French port and both received substantial bow damage. The 'Cote' immediately was sent to Dunkirk where her damaged bow visor was removed and her water-tight door was welded up. She recommenced service six days later looking a very strange sight and operated throughout the rest of the season as a stern loader.

As she was so close to retirement, SNCF considered not replacing the *Chantilly* and her twisted bow visor was deposited on the quayside at Calais. As the former Dieppe vessel *Villandry* was now available for use, she was quite capable of replacing the damaged ship.

More problems occurred shortly afterwards when the *St Christopher* went off service with engine problems and the *Horsa* was transferred from Folkestone to take her place. The *Villandry* was switched to cover her on the Folkestone – Boulogne route while Sealink chartered the Belgian ferry *Roi Baudouin* to cover the summer Dover – Boulogne link. Once again, a large fleet with spare ships had saved the day.

Early November saw the *St Anselm* off service and the transfer of the repaired *Chantilly* to the 'Flagship Service.' Once again the *Roi Baudouin* was available to cover the French ship on the Folkestone – Boulogne route. At this time an announcement was made concerning the closure of the Sealink service between Dover and Boulogne which for the previous few seasons had been operated only during summer peak periods. Ten years previously it had been the top link between England and France and now it was to be left to the newcomers on the route, P&O Normandy Ferries. A token Sealink service using the French train ferry *Saint Eloi* was to be offered on Saturday afternoons during the peak of the summer but no service operated under those conditions is likely to survive and this was no exception.

Towards the end of her career in the Dover Strait, the **Chantilly** *was relegated to the secondary services and is seen from the Belgian mail boat* **Prinses Paola** *leaving the Admiralty Pier linkspan for Calais with train-connected passengers. (Miles Cowsill)*

The *St Anselm* was back at Harland & Wolff after Christmas for £750,000 modifications to her after accommodation. To cover her roster, Sealink switched the fourth of the 'Saint' class from the Irish Sea and after a quick refit at Falmouth, the *St David* took up the route with the 13.00 to Calais on 31st March. The visitor had arrived late at Dover as she had been called in to cover for the failed Fishguard vessel *Stena Normandica* and just as the *St Anselm* was returning south to resume duties at Dover, the Stena vessel broke down again. The *St Anselm* was diverted to run the 14.45 to Rosslare on 28th March and finally arrived 'home' on the last day of the month. The following day the 'Christopher' returned to her builders for similar modifications and arrived back at Dover on 9th June after which the 'David' de-stored and sailed for Holyhead.

Following Sealink's decision to close the Calais – Folkestone route, a four-ship service between Dover and Calais commenced on 3rd June 1983. Due to the delay of the new *Champs Elysees*, the *Chantilly* filled the gap and certain train-connected services operated to and from the Admiralty Pier at Dover. Whilst the *Hengist* and *Horsa* were ideal for this type of traffic and had been purpose-built to handle it, the 'Saints' proved themselves to be totally inept at handling large numbers of luggage-laden foot passengers. Turn round times suffered, there was no where in the ships' accommodation to store the baggage and the narrowness of the Admiralty Pier linkspan prohibited them from serving as drive-through vessels as their sterns failed to fit. All lorries were therefore forced to reverse on board through the bow, which was not only unpopular but also very time consuming.

The £7 million double-deck ramp at Boulogne was finally ready for use in July 1984 and it was announced that the new SNCF ship would operate a daily 09.30 sailing from Dover with an 11.30 return.

The new *Champs Elysees* finally arrived at Calais at 10.30 on 30th September and the following day arrived at Boulogne for ramp tests. She then sailed from Calais to Dover on her maiden voyage at 07.30 on 4th October. The ship's capacity for 1,800 passengers, 300 cars or 53 x 15 metre lorry units was certainly impressive and she became the largest Sealink ferry operating across the Dover Strait.

The *Chantilly* was now retired from service and during the winter of 1984/85, Dover Harbour Board widened the Admiralty Pier linkspan to order to allow the larger units a proper port fit. The smaller ship was back on the Folkestone route to cover overhauls in January 1985 and during the summer season operated from the Western Docks (Admiralty Pier) to Calais before being withdrawn from service. She was switched to the Newhaven – Dieppe service in 1986 before sale to Greek owners Agapitos Bros. for whom she was renamed *Olympia* for service to Rhodes in 1987. Three years later she returned to the UK for rebuilding and became the *Europa Link* for G-T Link running between Gedser and Travemunde in the Baltic. Another three years elapsed before she was sold on to Polish interests becoming their *Baltavia* and three years later she sailed to Saudi Arabia becoming the *El Salam 93* for El Salam Shipping and entering the Red Sea pilgrim trade. She was later broken up at Alang.

The *Champs Elysees* took up her Dover – Boulogne sailings from 19th January 1985 running the 09.30 and 15.30 sailings until 20th March when the timings were changed to 10.15 and 16.30. However, the sailings were operated on Wednesdays and Saturdays only and with that type of infrequency it did not take long before the Boulogne service lost money. As from 1st July, the Wednesday sailings were cancelled and on 28th September, the *St David* slotted into the remaining Saturday runs. The ship had been brought back to Dover in March to run the Sealink Dover – Ostend service following the demise of the overnight service from Folkestone. The *Cote d'Azur* finally closed the Dover – Boulogne service in the New Year 1986.

PARTNERSHIPS

Overall, the partnership between the marine divisions of the nationalized railway companies of Britain and France worked extremely well. There were always financial constraints with the constant concern that new tonnage might coincide with the building of a Channel Tunnel and it is certainly true that without these constraints, Townsend Car Ferries/ Townsend Thoresen was able to grow and develop into a major operator and a real threat to the Sealink operatives. These also included Regie voor Maritiem Transport (RMT) on the Ostend – Dover link and the Zeeland Steamship Company (SMZ) on the Hook of Holland – Harwich route.

The denationalisation of Sealink UK Ltd in July 1984 was the start of a process which saw a gradual fragmentation of the Sealink consortium. Prior to this occurring, the 1984 season had seen the British Rail double-arrow logo removed from all funnels before the introduction of a brand new livery.

In readiness for privatisation in 1984, the local Sealink ships had their BR funnel arrow logos removed. Here is the **St Christopher** *in May that year. (John Hendy)*

Following her release from the Dover - Dunkirk train ferry link, the **Saint Eloi** *was chartered by SNCF to run rail-connected passenger services during summer 1988. She was revamped as the* **Channel Entente** *in the following year. (FotoFlite)*

The **Champs Elysees** *heading away from Calais in February 1990 prior to the SPN livery being introduced. (John Hendy)*

CHAPTER FOUR

DENATIONALISATION: THE SEA CONTAINERS YEARS

Sealink UK Ltd was sold for £66 million to the Bermuda-based Sea Containers under the Presidency of James Sherwood. There was an immediate and major reappraisal of all former Sealink UK crossings from which came expectations of new tonnage and new routes. Now trading as Sealink British Ferries, mistakes were made from the start, the promised new ships failed to materialise and former long-standing continental partners were alienated. The rather slow and gentle approach based upon mutual respect and understanding which perhaps characterised the years of nationalisation prior to 1984 was now subjected to the harsh realities of American-style business; and not everyone liked it.

We have already seen that in March 1985, Sealink British Ferries had transferred the *St David* from the Irish Sea to operate the Dover – Ostend service. On the opening of Folkestone as a ro-ro port in 1972, Sealink UK took a 15% share in the Belgian route and now under new ownership, announced that they wished to substantially increase their share.

This greatly upset the Belgians who in January 1986 did the unthinkable and entered into a trading agreement with arch-rivals Townsend Thoresen firmly shutting both Sealink British Ferries and the *St David* out of Ostend.

Sealink countered this with the introduction of a new freight service between Dover and Dunkirk West using the recently acquired deep-sea ro-ro vessels *Seafreight Freeway* and *Seafreight Highway*. Manning arrangements held up the introduction of the first ship and so the *St. Anselm* was used instead operating the 02.30, 10.30 and 18.30 sailings from Dover. When she went on refit during February, the French reactivated their ro-ro vessel *Transcontainer 1* until the 'Freeway' finally arrived on station in July.

As part of the new owners' policy of uprating and improving the onboard facilities of Sealink UK ships, both the *St Anselm* and the *St Christopher* were sent to Papenburg during the early part of the year to undergo refits costing in the region of £1.5 million. The improvements were a tremendous bonus to the route, the bar in particular coming in for special treatment to make it look more like a traditional English pub. The interior decorators' new pink carpets in the ships' after areas lasted weeks before something more suitable was found.

The 'Anselm' returned to Dover prematurely with fifty German workmen still on board as the SNCF ferry *Champs Elysees* was on strike and the *Cote d'Azur* was in dry dock at Dunkirk. She started again with the 11.15 on 14th March thereby missing by four days the former *Dover/Earl Siward* under tow from Cyprus to Newcastle for use as a nightclub.

With the *St Christopher* on refit, the *Vortigern* was brought back on 6th April again reappearing during October when the 'Christopher' was off service with crankshaft problems.

Rivals at Calais. The **St Christopher** *berthed alongside Townsend Thoresen's* **Free Enterprise VI** *shortly after the latter vessel was stretched for carrying more freight on the Zeebrugge service. (John Hendy)*

The **Cote d'Azur** *newly painted in the SPN livery in April 1990. (John Hendy)*

The **St Christopher** *(Captain E Venables) makes a fine sight as she leaves Calais at speed in her British Ferries livery. (John Hendy)*

During 1985, Sea Containers put forward proposals for their 'Channel Expressway', a road and rail tunnel under the Dover Strait. Had they been successful in their efforts, all 2,500 Sealink British Ferries workers ashore and afloat would have changed employment in support of the operation, thereby making the local Sealink fleet redundant. This news did little to endear the workforce to those in Sea Containers House who seemed more interested in a fixed link rather than developing the ferry services.

During October 1986, plans were being drawn up to jumboise the *St Anselm* and *St Christopher* by adding an extra deck and inserting either a 15 metre or 30 metre section amidships. It was calculated that the latter option would raise the ships' capacity by 25%. Financial constraints prevented the work from taking place during the winter of 1986/87 but a Sea Containers spokesman announced that the costs involved would be less than providing one new super-ferry. This was all in response to Townsend Thoresen's forthcoming 'Chunnel Beaters' *Pride of Dover* and *Pride of Calais* but nothing came of the idea and Sea Containers looked for other alternatives to compete with their rivals.

During the morning of the Great Storm (16th October 1987), hurricane force winds battered the south coast of England and Folkestone's *Hengist* was blown ashore just to the east of the port. The *St Christopher* was caught at sea during the height of the storm and was hit by seas of such energy that the ship's engines stopped and the vessel was plunged into darkness. A wave of such force had hit the steel door on her upper vehicle deck causing it to split open, flooding the vehicle decks and then the engine room. There was pandemonium on the car decks and using cranes and fork lift trucks, it eventually took three days to clear away the smashed and overturned vehicles. Fortunately the upper vehicle deck was empty but the ship had listed to almost 40 degrees and had had a narrow escape.

With Folkestone Harbour pier and station closed due to storm damage, the *Horsa* was switched to the Dover – Calais route in place of the damaged *St Christopher*.

The *St Anselm* and *St Christopher* received further internal modifications during early 1988 when their entire central sections in their main passenger decks were stripped out and completely rebuilt including the provision of a free-flow buffet.

The year 1988 saw the new SNCF train/ ro-ro vessel *Nord Pas-de-Calais* running freight on the Dover – Calais service between February and May after which she was finally able to use the new train ferry linkspan on Dover's Admiralty Pier extension which had been damaged during construction in the Great Storm of the previous October. With the new train-ferry operations now operational, between late May and late September the earlier generation Dunkirk train ferry *Saint Eloi* was now surplus to requirements and introduced on a twice-daily basis carrying foot passengers on the train-connected services from Dover Western Docks to Calais Maritime. The following year she was renamed *Channel Entente* before her sale to the Isle of Man Steam Packet Company in 1990 when she became their *King Orry* (VI). Having established herself as the most comfortable ferry in Manx service, she was sold out of service in 1998 becoming Moby Line's *Moby Love 2* and operating today (without the '2' suffix since 2002) between Piombino and Portoferraio. Between Dover and Calais, the *Channel Entente's* summer-only passenger services

With Folkestone Harbour closed after the Great Storm of October 1987, the **Horsa** was switched to run Dover - Calais vice the damaged **St Christopher**. The freighter **Seafreight Highway** lies on the Eastern Arm after having demolished the cafe at the end of the Prince of Wales' Pier. (John Hendy)

During a period of unprecedented industrial strikes involving Townsend Thoresen crews, in June 1988 Sealink chartered the Swedish ferry **Scandinavica** *to run to both Calais and Zeebrugge. (Ferry Publications Library)*

were duly taken by the SNCF ferry *Chartres*.

Then during a period of unprecedented industrial unrest at Dover and the subsequent lay-up of all the Townsend Thoresen fleet, a sixth Sealink vessel was introduced to absorb all the extra traffic on offer. This was the Swedish ferry *Scandinavica* (ex *Prinsessan Birgitta*, ex *Stena Scandinavica* – 9,017 gross tons, built 1974) which commenced her charter on 7th June running to Calais by day with an overnight run to Zeebrugge until 23rd August 1988.

On 13th October 1988, in part exchange for the unsuccessful *Seafreight Freeway* and *Seafreight Highway*, Sea Containers purchased the twin Bulgarian ro-ro ships *Tzarevetz* and *Trapezitza* for eventual conversion to compete with the new Townsend Thoresen 'Chunnel Beaters'. They were built at Malmo in 1980 and on acquisition one was immediately chartered to OT Africa Line and named *Fiesta* while the other was prepared for the Dover – Calais freight service and named *Channel Seaway*. The latter ship operated with a British crew between

The deep-sea freighter **Channel Seaway** *operated between Dover and Calais with a British crew during the 1988 season before being sent to Bremerhaven for conversion to the* **Fiesta**. *(John Hendy)*

Here is the ship at Bremerhaven as seen from her sister **Fiesta** *which became Sealink British Ferries'* **Fantasia**. *(John Hendy)*

May and October 1989 before being sent to Bremerhaven where she joined her sister for conversion to multi-purpose mode.

The work involved was the largest ever undertaken by Sealink. Some 2,000 tonnes of steel was added, the whole of their upper vehicle decks (each weighing 900 tonnes) were cut free and lowered by an average of 2 metres, a completely new deck (Deck 3) was built within the existing superstructures and extensive stability sponsons were added to the sides of the ships.

Added to this was their conversion to two-tier drive-through operations, the replacement of all life-saving appliances, the fitting of additional bow thrusters and new Bekker-type rudders. The new passenger accommodation for as many as 1,800 people was given a very high priority and Sea Containers appointed the American designer Warren Platner to complete his 'Floating World' concept.

During January 1990, the former *Channel Seaway* was transferred to French ownership and renamed *Fiesta* while her British sister became the *Fantasia*. The ships eventually entered service on 17th March (*Fantasia*) and 11th July (*Fiesta*) allowing the *Champs Elysees* to transfer to the Dieppe – Newhaven route.

In early March 1989, Stena Line of Gothenburg, purchased 8% of Sea Containers' shares and there commenced a protracted hostile takeover bid. This eventually ended on 31st May 1990 when in a deal worth £259 million, the Sealink business (minus the Isle of Wight and Hoverspeed operations) was acquired.

During the six years of Sea Containers ownership only four new vessels had been built (twin catamarans and twin car ferries for the Isle of Wight services). Sea Containers had promised much but had delivered very little. In terms of traffic across the Dover Strait, ground had been lost to Townsend Thoresen who were now very much in the ascendancy while the former Belgian partners in the Sealink consortium had been alienated resulting in the closure of the trade to Ostend. Quite clearly the injection of new capital and the expansion of the Sealink business as promised and expected following its privatisation now meant very little.

The **Fiesta** *in dry dock at Bremerhaven undergoing her conversion to become the* **Fantasia**. *These major rebuilds were in response to Townsend Thoresen's purpose-built 'Chunnel Beaters'. (John Hendy)*

*Finally in service; the **Fantasia** is seen as she originally appeared in her non-standard Sealink livery. The radical 'Brand World' of her interior spaces was the brainchild of the American designer Warren Platner. (John Hendy)*

*The **Fiesta** is photographed in the rather more restrained livery of SPN. Apart from the light of their passenger spaces, a feature of the twin ships was their excellent outside deck space. (John Hendy)*

CHAPTER FIVE

STENA LINE: THE END OF SEALINK

With Stena Line in control, further major evaluations of routes and tonnage were now forthcoming. With the *Fantasia* in service at Dover in 1990, local Sealink management had fought hard to retain the *St Anselm* which was switched to Folkestone – Boulogne in place of the *Horsa* which was sent to Holyhead for the season. Their confidence was rewarded with significant increases in passenger, car and freight traffic.

However, following a disastrous first year's trading, Stena Line found themselves in serious financial difficulties having paid Sea Containers way in excess of the company's market value. Having seriously misjudged the market by embarking on a Scandinavian cruise-style culture to encourage people to spend more money on board in a 'we are here to show you British how to run ferries' spree, Operation Benchmark was imposed to seek restructuring and economies. Their first victim was the Folkestone – Boulogne service which closed on the final day of 1991.

During 1991 the *St Christopher* was renamed *Stena Antrim* and was switched to the Stranraer – Larne route. She was not to return. In her place Sealink Stena had purchased the six-year-old Danish State Railways ferry *Peder Paars* (19,763 gross tons) for £40 million and after a further £6 million of modifications, duly placed her on the Dover – Calais service on 7th July. As the *Stena Invicta*, the vessel could accommodate as many as 2,000 passengers and 430 cars and she proved ideal for the tourist and day-trip market. However, as a freight carrier she was quite inadequate with space for just 36 x 15 metre units on her lower vehicle deck only. A second vessel was therefore required to cater mainly for the route's commercial traffic while allowing the *Stena Fantasia* and *Stena Invicta* to maximise the use of their on board facilities.

The £35 million *Stena Challenger* (18,253 gross tons) entered service on 27th June with capacity for 84 lorries and 500 passengers. She was actually on charter from Sealink Stena's parent company for £5 million per annum on which the daily interest alone was £8,000; she was always an expensive ship to operate. However, as part of Operation Benchmark, after less than six months in service the company decided to withdraw her at the close of 1991. This was hardly an example of forward planning from the new management but in the event she was removed to the Dunkirk West freight link before she was eventually restored to Dover – Calais when Sealink Stena and their French partners decided to operate a five-ship service as from May 1994.

During the winter of 1991-1992, both the *Stena Fantasia* and *Fiesta* were sent to Gothenburg to receive £12 million modifications which included two new higher rated bow thrusters in addition to a new azimuthing propulsion unit. With the latter fitted, nine single trips each day were made possible thereby increasing capacity on the route by 12.5%.

In November 1992, Sealink Stena Line officially became Stena Sealink Line, 'to reflect its Scandinavian ownership and quality service standards' so read the public relations material but this was simply an intermediate stage of a complete rebranding.

A most historic end of season event took place on Friday 24th September 1993 when the SNCF ferry *Chartres* made the final crossing of a passenger ship from Calais Maritime to Dover Western Docks (formerly Dover Marine) and the last Paris – London boat train was also operated. The ship was due to close the summer-only rail-connected service on the following day but instead she appeared at Portsmouth in support of the

The most unsuitable **Stena Invicta** *was introduced in 1991. Although her passenger spaces were of a high standard, her inability to carry freight on her upper vehicle deck was always a major operational drawback. (John Hendy)*

In order to carry the extra freight, Sealink Stena Line also introduced the underpowered ro-pax ferry **Stena Challenger**. *(John Hendy)*

After the Stena takeover, the **St Anselm** *was renamed* **Stena Cambria** *and sent to Holyhead. She was a frequent visitor to Dover and is seen leaving Calais in the Stena Sealink livery during March 1994. (John Hendy)*

CALAIS
DOVER

An impressive view of the **Stena Challenger** *as she appeared in the revised Stena Sealink livery during December 1994. (John Hendy)*

The **Stena Fantasia** *in her new owners' livery - now standardised to fit the rest of the fleet. (John Hendy)*

In late 1995 Stena dropped the Sealink name and repainted the former Sealink fleet in their own livery. Here is the **Stena Cambria**, *once more with red funnels, leaving through Dover's eastern exit. (John Hendy)*

The **Stena Fantasia** *approaches Dover wearing her newly painted Stena Line livery. (John Hendy)*

The **Stena Challenger** at Dover's berth 5. It was her grounding on the beach at Bleriot-Plage in September 1995 that brought forward Stena's plans to rebrand the Sealink fleet. (John Hendy)

The **Stena Empereur** (ex **Stena Jutlandica**) was another Baltic import which was found wanting on this most intensive of routes. She entered service at Dover in 1996 and boasted accommodation for 2,300 passengers. (John Hendy)

The fast craft **Stena Lynx III** at her Eastern Docks linkspan. Passengers disliked paying a premium for a faster crossing time with fewer on board facilities. (John Hendy)

yacht *La Poste* at the start of the Whitbread Round the World Yacht Race. The *Chartres* was almost immediately sold to Greece becoming the *Express Santorini* for services from Piraeus to Santorini until her withdrawal from service in 2006 since which time she has served for two summer seasons in the Azores.

It was eventually planned to rebrand Stena Sealink Line as from 1st January 1996 but after the underpowered *Stena Challenger* had been driven ashore onto the beach at Bleriot Plage near Calais by strong winds on 19th September 1995, a full refit took place on the Tyne and she re-entered service on 24th October in the full Stena Line livery. The unfortunate incident had simply advanced Stena's plans by two months.

The inevitable trading split between Stena Line and the French nationalised company Sealink SNAT occurred as from the first day of 1996 when both concerns sought to enlarge their respective fleets in order to both compete with each other and also P&O European Ferries.

The French operation is described in Chapter 10 but Stena reacted quickly by introducing the 78-metre fast craft *Stena Lynx II* (600 passengers, 130 cars) as from 13th February before she was abruptly removed to Gothenburg – Frederikshavn on 9th May. Following her 13,000 mile voyage from Hobart, the *Stena Lynx III* later reinstated the high speed service on 4th July. The £20 million craft was capable of 40 knots and could cross from pier to pier in 40 minutes although as berthing procedures could take a further 10 minutes, the company met with a degree of reluctance from their customers who saw little to be gained from saving 30 minutes in a vessel with far fewer facilities than all other vessels on the route. During the summer the smaller 74-metre *Stena Lynx* was made available to complement the fast crossings of her larger sister.

However, on 22nd March 1997 the *Stena Lynx III* was removed to the Newhaven – Dieppe link after the *Stena Cambria* (ex *St Anselm*) had made a welcome return to the Calais route to cover refit periods on 19th January.

In a move to further strengthen the Stena position, the largest ferry yet was now switched to the Calais link. This was the *Stena Empereur* (28,727 gross tons) which had entered service on the Gothenburg – Frederikshavn route in 1982 as the *Stena Jutlandica*. Accommodation was for as many as 2,300 passengers, 500 cars and 85 freight units and prior

to entering service, the ship received an £8 million overhaul which concentrated mainly on her duty-free shopping area and Calais port fit.

Entering service on 15th August 1997, the 'Empereur' replaced the *Stena Challenger* which was duly transferred to the Irish Sea. Even the new ship was not ideally suited to the Dover – Calais service. On her original route, her upper vehicle deck was loaded via side ramps but facilities at both Dover and Calais did not allow for this type of working. A single width door was cut into the 'Empereur's' forward superstructure thereby allowing slow double-deck working of freight vehicles of up to 4.7 metres high.

Thus Stena Line continued with a somewhat eclectic fleet that was proving to be no match for the purpose-built vessels operated on the route by P&O European Ferries. Of the two concerns, it was P&O who held the upper hand and who were proven market leaders on the Dover Strait. Whereas P&O catered mainly for the upper end of the passenger market and never failed to remind the public of their history and heritage as the leading British passenger shipping company, Stena's approach was far more basic with their intrusive music and fast food outlets. There really was no comparison – they were poles apart.

With profits dropping, Government permission to proceed with a Joint Venture was finally granted on 19th November 1997. The agreement covered not only the Dover – Calais link but also those between Dover – Zeebrugge and Newhaven – Dieppe. P&O would provide eight vessels and Stena five in addition to a fast craft. Voting rights would be 60 - 40 in favour of P&O.

In just 13 years, the Sealink organisation had been showered with broken promises and shattered by the failure of both Sea Containers and Stena Line to provide it with the right ships with which to compete. Privatisation plainly failed to bring the new investment that was required to allow the company to succeed on the most intensely operated route of all. New ships were provided but they were all second hand and all built for trades far removed from the Dover Strait. The last BR/ Sealink ships which were purpose-built for the Calais route remained the *St Anselm* and *St Christopher* in 1980/81. This in itself speaks volumes for the years of decline and under investment that followed.

Sealink, and all those who had worked for the company, deserved better.

CHAPTER SIX

TOWNSEND: FROM TRIUMPH TO TRAGEDY

Following its formation in January 1923, the Southern Railway Company's service linking Dover with Calais, carried an increasing number of motor cars which were craned on and off the ships by the lift on – lift off method. Those who chose to take their cars to the Continent were invariably wealthy but throughout the 1920s, a growing number of motor car enthusiasts began to cross the Dover Strait and found the Southern's charges to be exorbitant. The motoring community required a champion and were to find one in the form of Captain Stuart Townsend, whose Townsend Bros Shipping Ltd was involved in ship delivery, management and forwarding.

TAKING THE PLUNGE

Townsend had served as a Captain in the army during the Great War and it was then the practice to retain this title during a subsequent civilian career. He was one of many disgruntled motorists who believed that they were receiving a raw deal from the railway company to whom motor cars were at best a sure way of maximising profits and at worst a thorough inconvenience. Backed by 'The Autocar' magazine and the Civil Service Motoring Association, a feasibility study showed that it was possible to undercut the Southern's car rates by 50% and yet still make a profit and to use Townsend's own phrase, he decided to 'take the plunge.' Difficult as it may seem today, Townsend simply sought a guaranteed ten cars a day for a month and reasoned that it would take the Southern a month to realise what he was doing and another month to do something about it. His aim was simple – to force the Southern to reduce their rates and then cease trading. The railway company were then charging £5 15s 0d (£5.75) for a single Dover – Calais car journey whereas Townsend's rate was £2.

The Newcastle-owned steam collier *Artificer* (built in Dundee as the *Mercury* in 1905) was duly chartered for a period of one month, with an option for a second, in July 1928 and commenced service between the

Camber (at Dover's Eastern Docks) and the Quai Paul Devot at Calais. Both berths were on the opposite sides of their respective harbours from those used by the Southern Railway with all the attendant infrastructure which had accumulated throughout the years.

The *Artificer* (386 gross tons) could carry 15 cars but no more than 12 passengers and Townsend was struck by the number of drivers who had expressed a wish to actually travel with their vehicles rather than crossing the Channel by the Southern's comfortable and fast mail steamer service. The elderly collier took some 2 hours 30 minutes on passage and offered little in the way of passenger comforts. If food was required then they had to make their own arrangements with the ship's cook!

In the following year (1929), the *Artificer* was replaced on the service by the larger *Royal Firth* (411 gross tons, built at Hull in 1921) and Townsend Bros Car Ferries was formed. Profits for the first year of operation amounted to £80. As expected, the Southern responded with their own motorists' service, putting the chartered coasters *Dublin* and *Abington* on the Dover (Admiralty Pier) – Calais link while their new cargo vessel *Whitstable* operated a similar service between Folkestone and Boulogne. Their rates were lowered to match those of Townsend's service and then lowered still further in an attempt to undercut and force the new player out of business.

Townsend's base in the Eastern Docks at Dover was in the centre of a thriving ship-breaking industry and during the 1920s, it was kept particularly busy dismantling discarded units of the Royal Navy. There, under the noses of the Townsend board, the 'Town' class minesweeper HMS *Ford* was awaiting her turn for the breakers' torch when it was decided to inspect, and eventually purchase, the ship for conversion to a car ferry. The vessel was secured for £5,000 and she was promptly sent to Earle's Shipbuilding & Engineering Co at Hull where she was stripped and converted for civilian use to the design of Mr. Norman M. Dewar at a further cost of £14,000.

*The **Artificer** was chartered during the 1928 season to carry cars to Calais. She took two and a half hours on the crossing. The **Empress** or **Invicta** lies adjacent to the Gare Maritime. (AD Townsend)*

*The start of a transport revolution; during the 1936 French General Strike, the **Forde** presented her stern to the Quai Paul Devot and loaded via the drive on method. (AD Townsend)*

*The Townsend Channel Ferry **Forde** (Captain J Hume) entered service in 1930 and is seen leaving Dover during her brief post-war period of operation. She was withdrawn in 1949 and sold for further service in Gibraltar. (AD Townsend)*

HMS *Ford* had been built by Dunlop Bremner & Co at Port Glasgow in 1919 and had seen little service with the Royal Navy. She was 231 ft long with a beam of 28 ft 6 inches. Although several vessels of this type had previously been converted for civilian use, this was the first instance where one of them was required to carry a Steam 2 Passenger Certificate for short international voyages. Her hull was in excellent condition and she was built with more than enough bulkheads for the cross-Channel trade. A new steel car deck was added to allow petrol to be carried in cars for the first time. The ship remained a coal burner but interestingly she was built with a special 9 ft. by 6 ft. stern door which, it was hoped would drop down onto projected bridges (linkspans) which would connect ship with shore to counter the tidal variations at both ports.

As there was already a *Ford* in merchant service at that time, the new car carrier's name was amended and became *Forde*. She could carry 28 cars and 168 passengers and 34 crew although under a Steam 2 Limited Certificate, this could be raised to 307 passengers.

The new Townsend Channel Ferry commenced service on 15th April 1930, leaving Dover at 11.30 with arrival at Calais at 13.00 and a two-hour turn round in the French port.

From the start of the uprated service, Townsend stated that motorists would still prefer to drive their vehicles on board and it was hoped to have a special gangway at Dover later that year while arrangements on the French side would not be in use until 1931. Sadly, these schemes came to nothing and the ferry continued to be crane loaded. The service was an immediate success and although seasonal, in 1931 started as early as March. It was common practice throughout the 1930s to charter in coasters to handle the extra cars which the *Forde* could not carry while passengers would avail themselves of her superior accommodation.

In order to finance the conversion of the *Forde*, Townsend had floated a private company. Although the £1 shares were eventually to yield £15, public interest in the share issue was disappointing and in the event Townsend had to find most of the money himself. The company therefore remained private until for tax reasons it was floated again in 1956.

A three-week general strike in France started on 9th June 1936 and with no crane drivers available in Calais to lift the *Forde's* cars on and off, the shipping world was able to witness the simplicity of the drive on – drive off method of loading. Sailing from Dover to connect with the right level of tide at Calais, the *Forde* simply presented her stern to the quayside, lowered her stern gate and discharged in minutes. This was surely the start of a transport revolution and few who witnessed this pioneering event could have failed to be impressed.

With traffic blossoming, by 1936 the *Forde* was increasingly capacity constrained. Just before the outbreak of war, Townsend inspected the advanced drive – through Norwegian car ferry *Peter Wessel* but mechanical concerns saw his interest wane. The Board of Trade had already stated that the ship's bow door would have to be welded up for UK use.

With war in Europe having broken out, the *Forde* was sent to lay up in Poole Harbour before being requisitioned as a salvage vessel. Being of light construction she was far from ideal for this use and so appears to have served a quiet war.

With the Royal Navy leaving Dover Harbour in December 1946, the following April saw Townsend back in business using the chartered coaster *Cromarty Firth* before the *Forde* took up station some three weeks later. Capacity problems soon returned and the first cross-Channel car ferry was eventually retired on 18th October 1949. She was promptly

*The former frigate **Halladale** (Captain JE Dawson) took over the Townsend Channel Ferry in 1950 and maintained the link for the next eleven years. (FotoFlite)*

sold to MH Bland of Gibraltar and renamed *Gibel Tarik*, maintained the Tangier car ferry service until her boilers finally failed four years later and she was broken up in Malaga. Towards the end of her career, the ship starred with Sir Alec Guinness in the film, 'The Captain's Paradise' – a tale of a ferry Captain with a wife in both ports of call.

The *Forde* was replaced by another Royal Navy vessel, the 'River' class frigate HMS *Halladale* (K417). Built by A&J Inglis in Glasgow during 1944, she appears to have served just one commission before being laid aside at Portsmouth. The ship was purchased for £15,000, without inspection, in 1949 and was sent to the Rushbrooke yard of the Cork Drydock Co for a £77,000 conversion.

At 1,370 gross tons, the *Halladale* boasted accommodation for 55 cars and was driven by four Parsons steam turbines which at 20 knots, enabled her to make the passage in a little over an hour.

The *Halladale's* maiden voyage was carried out on 6th April 1950 and a year later she was able to berth at a second hand Callender-Hamilton bridge which Townsend had bought for use in assisting drive on – drive off operations at Calais in 1946. It was adapted for use at berth 3 and was first used by the *Halladale* on 27th June 1951, coming into regular use four days later.

Dover's Eastern Docks Car Ferry Terminal was not brought into official use until 30th June 1953 although the *Halladale* had been using the berths for two months previously.

GEORGE NOTT INDUSTRIES

In 1956, continued growth in traffic and the necessity for providing for death duties had prompted Townsend to go public but unfortunately, the share issue was launched on the very day that Egypt announced that the Suez Canal was to be nationalised; trade on the Stock Exchange slumped and very few shares were sold.

It so happened that in Coventry, a group of businessmen were at that time combing the Stock Market for a small company with large assets which they could transfer to their own interests. With assets of £500,000 ready for a time when a new ship was to be ordered, Mr George Nott of Monument Securities, Mr Roland Wickenden (his accountant and financial director) and Mr BW Stephenson (his stock broker) gained a controlling interest in the company and George Nott Industries took the helm. At an extraordinary general meeting of the shareholders in April 1957, Stuart Townsend and his fellow directors were voted off the board and so ended a notable era in the annals of cross-Channel history.

Had George Nott and his fellow directors had their way and stripped Townsend of its assets, 1957 would have in all probability been the final year of Townsend Bros Car Ferries and the *Halladale's* officers and crew certainly feared for the worse. There had been a time when Townsend had entered negotiations with British Railways regarding a takeover but their offer had been derisory and was rejected. How different things could have been.

Fortunately Nott was persuaded, in no little part by the *Halladale's* Captain Jack Dawson, to continue. Dawson told him that as Managing Director of Townsend Bros Car Ferries, he was now sitting on a gold mine and that the potential for money making was enormous.

The contrast between Stuart Townsend and George Nott could not have been greater. Townsend was a gentleman, polite and courteous with a genuine interest in ships and the sea and saw the company which bore his name as a family affair. Nott, on the other hand, was very much a self-made man with more than a few rough edges and who possessed a far more aggressive stance to people management, and with a turn of phrase to match. He had no knowledge of ships although he came to enjoy his position and the importance that it held. Captain Dawson remembered a time when, following a private visit to Birmingham, Nott tore him off a strip for not calling on him in Coventry!

The new board quickly looked to capitalise on their investment and in 1959, the year in which George Nott Industries acquired the whole of Townsend's share capital, the company illustrated their forward-looking views by taking on long-term charter from the Ministry of Transport, the twin screw tank landing ship *Empire Shearwater*.

Built at Sunderland in 1945, the ship was one of a large number of similar ships at lay-up in the Gareloch. The Atlantic Steam Navigation Company (which eventually came under the same ownership as Townsend) operated a small fleet of such vessels and served the Tilbury to Antwerp route across the southern North Sea. The charter of the 'Shearwater' offered a cut-rate alternative to the service offered by the ASN and a subsidiary company, European Ferries Ltd, was formed to operate it.

A special linkspan was erected at the foot of the Eastern Arm inside the Camber and amid much optimism, the new service started on 10th January 1959.

American army lorries and the antiques trade made use of the new service but the Calais customs were over-officious causing delays and ill feeling amongst the shippers. The service closed in June and at the end of September the ship was sent to lay up in the Medway.

In the last year of the *Halladale*, 27,487 cars and 86,744 passengers were carried. She finished service on 5th November 1961 and was later sold to Finnish owners for £42,000. She was named firstly as the *Norden* and then the *Turist Expressen* for work in the Baltic before a further sale in late in 1962 to Venezuelan owners Ferryboats Margarita for coastal work across the mouth of Lake Maracaibo where as the *Ferrymar III* she lasted for a further eleven years. Her hulk was not broken up until 1987.

For her final few years in service at Dover, the *Halladale* had been refitted at Verschure in Amsterdam and company officials had met and come to an understanding with representatives of their associates NV

Werf Gusto of Schiedam concerning a new ship which would be constructed at their yard.

Naval Architect James Ayres incorporated some new and innovative ideas in his design which included diesel engines, twin funnels, open-plan accommodation and, should the long-expected freight boom ever take off, a higher than usual vehicle deck headroom of 14 ft.

The *Free Enterprise* was unusually broad in the beam compared with her length and her flared bow and pyramidal superstructure gave her something of a yacht-like appearance. She was certainly a unique little vessel which within her 18-year career with the company was to see a complete revolution in cross-Channel ship design.

Costing £1 million, the keel of the *Free Enterprise* was laid on 7th August 1961 and was launched eight months later by Mrs Bernice Nott on 2nd February 1962. Her maiden voyage was scheduled for 12th April but delays at the builders saw this date modified to 22nd April.

THE FREE ENTERPRISE FLEET

In her first season, the *Free Enterprise* carried 55,000 cars, almost double that carried by the *Halladale* in 1961. Services were still operated on a seasonal basis and consisted mainly of holiday tourist traffic. A joint service to Calais was operated during the winter months with SNCF's car ferry *Compiegne*.

However, it was not long before the *Free Enterprise II* was being planned and she became the first British-owned drive through ferry. Launched at Schiedam on 29th January 1965, the £1.3 million vessel was designed with a lower than usual main vehicle deck height as the expected surge in lorry traffic had not materialised. This was soon to cause the ship major operational problems and although she remained an excellent car and caravan shipper, her lack of headroom meant that she was the least successful of the 'Free Enterprise' series of eight ships. At 4,122 gross tons, she was the largest British car ferry and completed her maiden voyage to Calais on 22nd May.

The first great change to the established Townsend service occurred

An unsuccessful experiment; in 1959, Townsend chartered the former tank landing craft **Empire Shearwater** *and ran her on a Dover - Calais freight service. Her time had not yet come and she was soon withdrawn. (FotoFlite)*

The green-hulled **Free Enterprise** *(Captain JE Dawson) entered service in 1962 and soon established herself as an excellent car carrier with extra headroom for freight, should it ever materialise. (John Hendy)*

on 17th March 1966 when the *Free Enterprise II* opened a new service to the Belgian port of Zeebrugge. The 4-hour crossing originally used a berth inside the entrance of the Baudouin Canal. However, it was not until the appearance of the *Free Enterprise III* in July 1966 that freight traffic at last started to gather pace. With accommodation for 1,200 passengers and 221 cars, or lorry space for 14 units in addition to 102 cars, growth on the Belgian route was dramatic. During 1966 just 2,687 lorries were carried by the three Townsend ferries while 1967 saw this leap to 17,250 – an increase of 600%, three-quarters of which were carried on the Zeebrugge route.

Townsend Car Ferries ('Bros' had been dropped from their title in 1965) initially showed interest in the developing cross-Channel hovercraft trade and on 30th April 1966 started operating the SRN-6 *Britannia* (024) between the Camber at Dover Eastern Docks and Calais. Unfortunately weather and technical problems beset the project and the craft completed her final crossing on 26th September. Although she gave off the beach joy rides from a number of other Kentish resorts during 1967, the *Britannia* was eventually returned to the British Hovercraft Corporation and Townsend decided not to follow up their option on the car carrying SRN-4.

The *Free Enterprise IV* set the trend for the five remaining 'Free Enterprise' series. Boasting accommodation for 260 cars (or 24 lorries) and 1,132 passengers her layout was extremely successful and was continued until a complete reassessment was required for the 1980 season. She was launched on 1st March 1969 and entered service to Zeebrugge on 1st June. Her arrival saw the *Free Enterprise II* offered for sale but in the event she was switched to offer an extra seasonal Southampton – Cherbourg crossing operating with the former Thoresen

Car Ferries. George Nott Industries had acquired Thoresen in the previous year creating the European Ferries Group (EFG).

The *Free Enterprise V* entered service on the Zeebrugge route on 31st May 1970 while the *Free Enterprise VI* followed in late June 1972 and the *Free Enterprise VII* came on station on 26th February 1973. The final three of the series were built with the more powerful Stork-Werkspoor engines rather than the Smit MAN engines of the earlier ships. A further modification was the installation of fin stabilisers rather than the passive 'flume' stabilisation systems of the previous four ships.

The final ship of the series was the *Free Enterprise VIII* which was built at the Verolme Shipyard at Alblasserdam and the only one of the 'Free Enterprise' class not to be delivered with a pale green hull which had failed to show up the company name when written along it. A darker

Dover Eastern Docks with the **Lord Warden** *off service in the lay-by berth, the* **Free Enterprise** *leaving berth 1 and the* **Dover** *in berth 2. (John Hendy)*

In 1965, the **Free Enterprise** *received the suffix 'I' in readiness for the 'FE II'. (FotoFlite)*

Dressed overall at Calais in May 1965, the new **Free Enterprise II** *had just opened the port's second linkspan. The 'FE I' lies alongside at the original berth. (John Hendy)*

Townsend's **Free Enterprise II** *was the first British registered drive-through car ferry and entered service in 1965. Her lack of headroom made her the least successful of the 'Free Enterprise' series. (FotoFlite)*

*The **Free Enterprise IV** leaving Calais after the application of a darker green hull colour and new funnel TTF logo in 1974. The lighter shade of green had failed to show the company trade name along the hull. (AG Jones)*

*The **Free Enterprise V** at Calais in her Thoresen orange hull which the fleet received from 1976. Following the Zeebrugge disaster eleven years later, hulls became dark P&O blue. (AG Jones)*

*In June and July 1981 the **Free Enterprise III** was chartered by British Rail to operate the train-connected link from Dover Admiralty Pier to Calais and Boulogne. This was in place of the **Caledonian Princess** which had been recalled to the Channel Islands routes. (AG Jones)*

The **Free Enterprise VII** *at lay-up on the Granville Dock's Cross Wall on Boxing Day 1984. (AG Jones)*

green hull was therefore adopted until in 1976, Thoresen orange became the order of the day. The 'FE VIII' was 6 metres longer than her sisters and Captain Dawson persuaded his Marine Superintendent that she was too long to fit Calais as a result of which, in her earlier days she was always associated with the Belgian route. With the new ship in service to Zeebrugge on 18th July 1974, the 'FE III' was switched to operate the Cairnryan – Larne route while the 'FE I' moved to the North Channel in the following year. She, in turn, was followed there by the 'FE IV' in 1976 and such was her success that she remained for ten years.

Between 1974 and 1979, all eight 'Free Enterprises' were in service together (see 'The Townsend Eight' – Ferry Publications) but towards the end of this period, the *Free Enterprise I* was only being used at peak periods and operated her final crossing from Dover to Calais on Christmas Eve 1979 before her sale to Ventouris Ferries of Greece in the following February. There she operated as the *Kimolos* before sale and

becoming the *Ergina* in 1993. Two years later she became the *Methodia II* and in 1997 the *Kallisti* for use as a day cruiser carrying passengers from Crete to the volcanic island of Santorini. She became the *Okeanis* in 2006. At the time of writing, the 'FE1' was still afloat at anchor in Elefsis Bay (Greece) after having spent longer in the Aegean than she did in the Dover Strait.

Group Technical Director James Ayres had searched European shipyards for a standard design of roll on – roll off ship which could be adopted for Townsend Thoresen use on the company's routes. Schichau Unterweser AG (SUAG) at Bremerhaven subsequently built three ships, the *European Gateway* for Felixstowe and the *European Trader* and *European Clearway* for Dover – Zeebrugge in 1975/76. The latter ships frequently appeared on the Dover – Calais link and were joined by a modified *European Enterprise* in 1977. Each could carry 1,000 metres of freight and held passenger certificates for 132 drivers.

The freighter **European Trader** *(Captain G Saunders) at number 5, the first of the new linkspans in the outer harbour which were built for the arrival of the 'Spirit' class in 1980. (Calais Chamber of Commerce)*

The **Free Enterprise VIII** *(Captain JE Dawson) in Dover's berth 4 in June 1979. The ship was associated with the Zeebrugge route for most of her earlier career, it being believed that her extra length would make her unsuitable for Calais. This proved to be a myth. (John Hendy)*

The third of the record-breaking 'Spirit' class ferries was the **Pride of Free Enterprise** *(Captain RP Blowers) which is seen alongside HMS* **Belfast** *in the Pool of London shortly after entering service. (John Hendy collection)*

THE FINAL YEARS

Townsend Thoresen's final decade started with the promise of the most intensive cross-Channel war in the history of the service.

Throughout the 1950s and 1960s, British Railways had concentrated their car ferry services on the Dover – Boulogne route. However, since 1970, they had directed their considerable resources at Calais where they were in direct competition with Townsend Thoresen.

With freight capacity at a premium on all routes, the Sealink consortium of British Rail and French partners SNCF Armement Naval had promised three new ferries with double freight decks and duly introduced the *St Anselm, St Christopher* and *Cote d'Azur* in 1980/81. All three were late being delivered. Townsend Thoresen's contribution was the three 'Spirit' class ships from SUAG at Bremerhaven.

The three ships were unlike anything else that the British ferry industry had ever witnessed. Their appearance was certainly unconventional but their technical performance was extremely impressive allowing them to operate an unprecedented five round trips each day working at speeds which the Dover – Calais route had not witnessed for very many years.

Under the command of the late Captain Oliver Elsom, the *Spirit of Free Enterprise* left Dover on her maiden voyage on 14th January 1980. Following her 53 minute 49 second dash from pier-to-pier, the 'SOFE,' as she was nicknamed, introduced 'The Blue Riband Route' which Townsend Thoresen now used to advertise the Dover – Calais crossing.

The *Herald of Free Enterprise* followed on 29th May before she broke her sister's pier-to-pier crossing time by clocking 52 minutes 53 seconds in a force 8 gale of wind. The trio was completed with the arrival of the *Pride of Free Enterprise* on 23rd November. The following February she broke her sister's record by four seconds.

The new record-breaking ships saw the end of the first three 'Free Enterprise' ships. The 'FE II' briefly returned to the Calais route in April and May 1980 before spending a final season on the Portsmouth – Cherbourg link. She was sold to Navarma/ Moby Lines and became their *Moby Blu* for a service linking Elba and Piombino before being broken in India in 2004. As for the 'FE III', she was sold to Maltese owners and renamed *Tamira* in 1984 but was immediately resold to the Isle of Man Steam Packet Company becoming their *Mona's Isle* for the Douglas – Heysham link. Sadly, she proved to be an operational disaster for the Manx company who withdrew her after only six months in service with serious deadweight problems. Thereafter she was sold to Egyptian owners Sadaka Shipping for whom she was renamed *Al Fahad*. Engaged in the Red Sea pilgrim trade, the ship was abandoned near Jeddah, Saudi Arabia, during 1998 after developing a heavy list.

With even more freight space required on the Zeebrugge link, in 1985

The stretched **Free Enterprise VI** *at berth 4 at Calais. By this time the original vehicle ferry berth (number 3) had been resited towards the Gare Maritime. (John Hendy)*

Spirit of Free Enterprise. *(FotoFlite)*

*The ill-fated **Herald of Free Enterprise** is seen arriving at Dover from Calais during her second year in service. The second of the 'Spirit' class, the trio reintroduced 60-minute crossings of the Dover Strait. (John Hendy)*

both the 'FE VI' and 'FE VII' were sent back to SUAG at Bremerhaven for extensive rebuilds which enabled them to carry 60 lorries instead of 24. The 'FE V' was returned to Dover from Portsmouth during this period (she had been serving the Hampshire port since 1982) and on the return of the 'stretched' sisters both made occasional sailings to Calais.

After the present plans for a fixed-Channel link were announced, Townsend Thoresen unveiled their own plans for the 'Chunnel Beaters' – two giant ferries which they claimed would threaten the viability of the tunnel. The contract was awarded to SUAG at Bremen and a competition

was held amongst the local staff to suggest suitable names; the £85 million twins were named *Pride of Dover* and *Pride of Calais*.

These were bleak times for the European Ferries Group. After having acquired substantial holdings in the US property market, a drop in oil prices had a disastrous effect on the company assets. In January 1986, the P&O Group acquired a controlling interest in a company holding almost 21% of the EFG shares and from that time its future was in doubt. Market analysts indicated that the company had lost its direction ever since the untimely deaths of Managing Directors Roland Wickenden, in 1972, and

*The **Pride of Dover** fitting out at Bremerhaven. Following the Zeebrugge disaster, her entry into service in 1987 was a very low-key affair but she has proved to be a most successful vessel. (John Hendy collection)*

*The **Spirit of Free Enterprise** (Captain O Elsom) is seen off Calais with Townsend Thoresen's new funnel logo in November 1985. (John Hendy)*

then his brother Keith in 1983, and so in December 1986, the inevitable takeover occurred.

The loss of the *Herald of Free Enterprise* off Zeebrugge on the night of 6th March 1987 was a tragedy which should never have occurred and which represented Dover's worst ever ferry disaster. The death toll that evening came to 193 passengers and crew who are all remembered in a stained glass window in Dover Parish Church.

It had been the company's intention to transfer the 'Herald' to the Zeebrugge link on a full-time basis following the entry into service of the two new 'Chunnel Beaters' but now a cloud descended and the entry into service of the new ships was that of quiet restraint rather than one of

joyous happiness. The £46 million *Pride of Dover* boasted capacity for 2,290 passengers and 650 cars (or 100 x 15 metre lorries) and under the command of Captain John Martin, operated her maiden voyage on 2nd June 1987. She originally entered service with an orange Townsend Thoresen hull but with an interim P&O pale blue funnel.

With the Calais route a ship down following the loss of the 'Herald', the *Free Enterprise V* was transferred from the Boulogne service while the spare Sealink vessel *Vortigern* was chartered to run the secondary link in her place. The delivery of the new *Pride of Dover* saw the restoration of the status quo.

*The **Pride of Dover** (Captain J Martin) making her very first departure from Dover sailing through the western exit for trials at Calais. (John Hendy)*

CHAPTER SEVEN

P&O EUROPEAN FERRIES: A NEW BEGINNING

Even before the creation of P&O European Ferries in October 1987, the new management had set out to distance itself from the 'sloppy practices' which had been highlighted at the Sheen enquiry into the loss of the 'Herald'.

Ships' funnels were immediately painted in P&O pale blue with the company house flag while the familiar 'Free Enterprise' names were changed to those of towns in East Kent. The *Pride of Free Enterprise* was switched to the Zeebrugge link and thus given a Belgian name as a gesture of thanks for the magnificent local efforts made in the aftermath of the 'Herald's' loss. The Dover fleet was renamed thus:

Townsend Thoresen names	P&O European Ferries names
Free Enterprise V	*Pride of Hythe*
Free Enterprise VI	*Pride of Sandwich* (later *Pride of Ailsa*)
Free Enterprise VII	*Pride of Walmer* (later *Pride of Rathlin*)
Free Enterprise VIII	*Pride of Canterbury*
Spirit of Free Enterprise	*Pride of Kent*
Pride of Free Enterprise	*Pride of Bruges*
European Trader	*European Trader*
European Clearway	*European Clearway*
European Enterprise	*European Endeavour.*

On the creation of P&O European Ferries during October, all ships received dark blue hulls and funnels with the P&O house flag on the latter. The *Pride of Calais* (Captain Bob Blowers) entered service on 4th December allowing the *Free Enterprise IV* to stand down from the Boulogne service. With the *Pride of Bruges* moving to the Zeebrugge route, the 'FE VIII'/ *Pride of Canterbury* was then switched to operate the Boulogne link with the 'FE V'/ *Pride of Hythe*. As for the 'FE IV', she was sold to G-T Link for Baltic service linking Gedser and Travemunde where she was renamed *Falster Link*. Then, in 1998 she was sold to the Egyptian company El Salam Maritime taking up the Red Sea pilgrim trade as the *Tag Al Salam* (meaning 'Crown of Peace') until being sold for scrap in 2006.

With the new ships in service, a new era of cross-Channel travel had begun. Further investment totalling some £235 million followed between 1991-93. Three new 'Super-European' class freighters were built for the Zeebrugge link (*European Seaway, European Pathway* and *European Highway*) while a fourth vessel, originally to be named *European Causeway*, was converted on the stocks to become the *Pride of Burgundy* which provided additional tonnage for the Calais link. The ship entered service on 5th April 1993 bringing the Dover – Calais fleet up to five and enabling the company to offer their own 'Channel Shuttle' a whole year before the tunnel opened. In a further boost to passenger comfort, the fitting of the excellent Club Class lounges on all passenger ships recreated a First Class standard which was light years away from the tunnel that, in the words of the late Brian Langford, simply offered its customers 'a light bulb and a loo'.

The *Pride of Kent* had been sent to Palermo (Sicily) for refurbishment and stretching by 31.5 metres in order to make her compatible with the

Illustrating the growth in size of ferries within a period of 13 years. The **Pride of Bruges** *(ex* **Pride of Free Enterprise***) leaves Dover for Zeebrugge while the* **Pride of Burgundy** *loads for Calais. (John Hendy)*

*The **Pride of Calais** (Captain RP Blowers) approaching Calais. Entering service in December 1987, the second of Townsend Thoresen's 'Chunnel Beaters' has served her owners well during her career on the Dover Strait. (John Hendy)*

*The **European Endeavour** (ex **European Enterprise**) was the fourth of a quartet of ro-ro vessels built by SUAG at Bremerhaven and the only one with modifications made by her owners. She finished her career on the North Channel and currently operates on the Ostend - Ramsgate link. (John Hendy)*

The **Pride of Bruges** (Captain V Ridges) back on the Calais route and heading for Dover. (John Hendy)

new 'Dover' and 'Calais'. Although her accommodation now boasted room for 1,850 passengers and 460 cars (or 64 x 15 metre lorries), operationally the stretching was not the success it was hoped for and sister ship the *Pride of Bruges* did not follow suit.

With the focus of operation on the shortest sea crossing, the passenger service to Zeebrugge closed on 31st December 1991 and it was decided to close the Boulogne route on 4th January 1993. The *Pride of Hythe* was sold to Slovenian operators Denval and became their *Laburnum*. After a period in the Adriatic operating from Italy to Albania and then Montenegro, in 2001 she was surprisingly switched to TransEuropa Shipping Line's Ostend – Ramsgate service on which she operated for 18 months. She was then chartered to Comanav running as the *Tadla* on the long Genoa – Tangier link and then from Naples to Nador before being offered for sale in 2005. In 2006 she operated for Ferrimaroc on their Almeria – Nador route before sale to Veronica Line in 2007 when she worked the Otranto – Durres (Albania) link. In 2008 she was operating as the *Veronica Line* on a service from Brindisi to the Albanian port of Vlore.

On the closure of the Boulogne link, the *Pride of Canterbury* was quickly sold to GA Ferries for whom she operates today as the *Romilda*.

Following the closure of the Zeebrugge route to passengers and the entry into service of the new freighters, the former *Pride of Sandwich* and *Pride of Walmer* were duly switched to the North Channel route and renamed *Pride of Ailsa* and *Pride of Rathlin*. The former completed service

in June 1993 before her sale to Egyptian owners El Salam Shipping for whom she was renamed *Pride of Al Salam 95* for a 40-hour service in the Red Sea carrying pilgrims between Egypt and Saudi Arabia. In this role her passenger certificate was raised from 650 to 2,500 but her end was sudden when at Suez on 17th October 2005 she was rammed and sunk by a Cypriot cargo ship. All but a few of the 1,466 passengers on board managed to escape to the cargo ship but once the two ships had separated, the former 'FE VI' went down in three and a half minutes with a loss of eleven lives.

As for the *Pride of Rathlin* (ex *Pride of Walmer*), she continued at Larne until 2000, completing her career as the final 'Free Enterprise' on 11th September. She was duly sold to Indonesian owners, Sungi Budi of Jakarta and renamed *BSP III* for service linking the islands of Java and Sumatra.

Portsmouth's **Pride of Winchester** at Calais during a period of winter reliefs in 1989. (John Hendy)

The **European Seaway** was the lead ship in a series of four freighters built for the Zeebrugge link. The last of the group was converted to become the **Pride of Burgundy**. (John Hendy)

CHAPTER EIGHT

P&O AND STENA: THE JOINT VENTURE

The Joint Venture between P&O European Ferries and Stena Line represents a brief but significant chapter in the annals of the Dover – Calais crossing. The new service was officially launched in March 1998 and the ships involved were:

Previous name	New name	Notes
Pride of Dover	P&OSL Dover	
Pride of Calais	P&OSL Calais	
Pride of Kent	P&OSL Kent	PO Kent in 2002
Pride of Bruges	P&OSL Picardy	
Pride of Burgundy	P&OSL Burgundy	
European Seaway		Zeebrugge freight
European Pathway		Zeebrugge freight
European Highway		Zeebrugge freight
Stena Empereur	P&OSL Provence	
Stena Fantasia	P&OSL Canterbury	PO Canterbury in 2002
Stena Invicta		Chartered – sold May 2000
Stena Cambria		Sold February 1999
Stena Antrim		Sold June 1998
Elite		Fast craft. Returned to Stena Oct 1998.

There was an immediate need to 'harmonise' the two fleets and to provide a new on board experience. Operationally, it was planned to offer a 'seamless' service with seven ships offering departures every 45 minutes between 08.00 and midnight.

One of the first tasks concerned the former *Stena Empereur* which required new generators in order to provide more light in what was always a rather gloomy ship. She was fast on passage but not being built for the route, performed badly when manoeuvring in port so that attention to her bow-thrust units was also required.

The new company sought to create a 'brand world' for the fleet which would see standardised fittings and fixtures throughout. The Langan's Brasseries, which had become so popular throughout the P&O fleet, were now fitted to the former Stena units as were various other outlets selling a variety of food and beverages. Club Class Lounges, in which discerning passengers could escape the busy spaces elsewhere on board, were also introduced and the two remaining Stena ships on Dover – Calais were most certainly improved as a result of all this.

It was initially envisaged that the *Pride of Bruges* would be transferred to operate the Newhaven – Dieppe link and she carried out trials at both ports. There was some concern that her draft might be a problem in the River Ouse at low water and in the event, the *Stena Cambria* was used to operate the service with the former *Stena Lynx III*, now renamed *Elite*. The fast craft was promptly dispensed with as being unreliable and prone to delays and on the last day of January 1999, the *Stena Cambria* closed the link and was offered for sale.

Due to the *Stena Invicta's* poor freight capacity, she was not to work for the new company but was laid up on 18th February 1998 before being chartered for the season to Silja Line operating in the Gulf of Bothnia and marketed as the *Wasa Jubilee*. She later laid up in Zeebrugge but was chartered to Stena for Irish Sea winter reliefs before being sold to Color Line in May 2000, becoming their *Color Viking* on the Sandefjord to Stromstad service across Oslofjord.

The P&O and Stena joint house flag as worn on the funnel of the **P&OSL Aquitaine**. *(John Hendy)*

The **Stena Empereur** *was renamed* **P&OSL Provence** *and much work was done to improve her mechanical and on board performance. (John Hendy)*

The **P&OSL Kent** *at Calais. The former* **Spirit of Free Enterprise** *was stretched by 31.5 metres at Palermo in 1991-92; the work cost £29 million. (John Hendy)*

The **P&OSL Aquitaine** *was built as the Ostend - Dover Line's* **Prins Filip** *and was chartered to P&O Stena Line by a Stena Line subsidiary. She is pictured swinging inside the eastern entrance of Dover Harbour. (John Hendy)*

The **P&OSL Picardy** *(ex* **Pride of Bruges***) was withdrawn from service following the acquisition of the* **P&OSL Aquitaine***. She is seen leaving Calais - notice the SeaCat berth further up the harbour. The ferry serves today on the Ostend - Ramsgate link. (John Hendy)*

Leaving Dover Harbour in the freighter **European Seaway** *as the* **P&OSL Dover** *manoeuvres in the harbour to go astern. The* **SeaFrance Renoir** *and* **P&OSL Kent** *are at the berths. (John Hendy)*

The ship had spent less than seven years at Dover but her vehicle deck layout belonged to an earlier generation of ferry and, in spite of her fine passenger spaces she was always going to struggle on this most competitive of routes.

Neither did the *Stena Antrim* (ex *St Christopher*) ever operate for the Joint Venture. She finished her days on the Newhaven – Dieppe route and after being withdrawn and replaced by her sister on 24th April 1998, she sailed to Zeebrugge to lay up before being sold to Limadet of Morocco on 11th June. She was renamed *Ibn Batouta* for service between Algeciras and Tangiers.

As for the *Stena Cambria*, after closing the Dieppe route, she was also laid at Zeebrugge before being purchased by Spanish owners Umafisa. Renamed *Isla de Botafoc*, she was handed over on 18th February and used on the Barcelona – Ibiza service.

The French crews from the 'Cambria' were transferred to the freighter *European Pathway* which was at that time laid up without a gearbox that had been transferred to the *P&OSL Burgundy*. With the Zeebrugge service a ship short, it was decided take a four month charter of the *Stena Royal*, the former *Prins Filip* of the Ostend – Ramsgate Line which had lain at Dunkirk East ever since the closure of the Belgian Government's service in February 1997. It was soon realised that the *Stena Royal* presented the company with a golden opportunity to improve standards on their Calais route and after she had entered service on 20th November 1998, the charter was quickly extended to seven years - ending on 31st December 2005. An extensive overhaul followed and renamed *P&OSL Aquitaine,* the ferry took up service to Calais in a freight mode on 7th November 1999, and was fully operational two days later. Work on her interior was still going on at that time and as her finish was the first indication of the type of standard which the public might expect from the Joint Venture, it was subjected to close scrutiny. Not surprisingly, the result was somewhere in between: an improvement on Stena but certainly below the standard expected of P&O.

Once the annual refits had been completed, the *P&OSL Picardy* was withdrawn from service and offered for sale as from 3rd February 2000 when she was operating on the Zeebrugge freight link. The ship today operates from Ramsgate to Ostend as TransEuropa Ferries' *Oleander*.

On 27th April 2000, the *P&OSL Aquitaine* was involved in a heavy collision with berth 7 at Calais when her engines failed to reverse to slow her forward momentum. Several passengers were injured by falling down companionways, and with the ship's bow badly damaged, it took some seven hours to remove all her traffic. While the 'Aquitaine' was being repaired at Falmouth, the Zeebrugge freighter *European Seaway* was diverted to run day services to Calais.

On 21st June, the 'Burgundy' sailed up the Thames as far as Deptford where she was involved in a function to celebrate her association with the Burgundy region. Her upper vehicle deck was converted into a dining room for 500 guests.

It was announced during spring 2002 that the Joint Venture was to end. P&O were invited to purchase Stena's 40% for £150 million while P&O's involvement with Felixstowe would also be terminated with Stena taking over the route and its elderly ro-ro ships. For Stena, it was an opportunity to improve their freight services in the North Sea while for P&O, it was a chance to capitalise on the high-capacity short-sea business that it knew best. The agreement was cleared by the European Commission on 8th August and during October, P&O acquired Stena's share of the business.

The Joint Venture's four years effectively saw the end of the route's former railway/ Sealink heritage although ex Stena personnel remained with P&O Ferries.

The **P&OSL Dover** *chases the freighter* **European Seaway** *into Calais Harbour. (John Hendy)*

CHAPTER NINE

P&O FERRIES: KEEPING UP TRADITION

During August 2002, P&O Ferries announced details of what they termed, 'The Darwin Project'. With the Dover – Zeebrugge service due to close on 15th December, the freighters *European Pathway* and *European Highway* were to undergo conversion to passenger ships for the Dover – Calais link.

The 'Pathway' completed service at Zeebrugge on 22nd April leaving it to the 'Highway' to close the route. Both were sent to Lloyd Werft at Bremerhaven where the work was carried out throughout the winter of 2002-03. Their profiles were completely changed and passenger capacity was raised from 200 to 2,000.

The 'Pathway' was renamed *Pride of Canterbury* while the 'Highway' became *Pride of Kent* and they re-entered service at Dover on 12th May and 14th June 2003. The ships were renamed by Lady Helen Stewart (wife of former racing driver Sir Jackie Stewart) in a joint ceremony on the Admiralty Pier extension on the evening of 28th June.

The *PO Canterbury* (as she was briefly styled) duly completed her service on 14th May and so it may be seen that for two days, there were two ships with almost the same names in service together. The former *Fantasia* was then sent to Dunkirk East to lay up and following her sale in October 2003 finally sailed to GA Ferries of Greece as the *Alkmini A* in the following March. Hers was but the briefest stay in the Aegean and after the 2004 season running across the Adriatic from Brindisi to Igoumenitsa, in September she was quickly resold to Polferries who in

the following February introduced her on the cross-Baltic service from Swinoujscie to Ystad as the *Wawel*.

The rest of the P&O fleet underwent a minor livery change during the winter period of 2002 – 2003 which involved the lowering of the blue hull paint. This tended to give the impression of a rather top-heavy appearance but allowed the application of the company website and 'P&O' in rather larger letters across the enlarged white superstructures. Company flags were also enlarged on the funnels and now filled their blue backgrounds.

With the new *Pride of Kent* in service, the old *PO Kent* (ex *Spirit of Free Enterprise*) duly finished service on 7th June 2003. She too was laid up in Dunkirk East and also passed to GA Ferries who renamed her *Anthi Marina* for the lengthy service from Piraeus to Kos and Rhodes. She left Dunkirk on 9th August and after conversion (which included a new bow section) commenced service for her new owners on 20th December.

The winter period of 2003 – 2004 was an extremely taxing period for P&O Ferries who, as part of a wide ranging business review, now looked to make savings of £15 million. The threat of international terrorism coupled with passenger traffic being lost to the airlines was given as the cause of the retrenchment as the remaining freighter *European Seaway* was withdrawn from service on 1st January 2004 and the *Pride of Burgundy* became freight-only as from 1st March. Neither did the rest of the fleet escape the essential cuts as from the start of 2004 most on board services were closed at night.

The **Pride of Dover** *storms into Calais, complete with her newly enclosed bridge wings, on a summer's day in August 2003. (John Hendy)*

The **Pride of Aquitaine** (*Captain J Hall*) *at berth 3, Dover Eastern Docks. Her modified 'Joint Venture' interior proved something of a disappointment. (John Hendy)*

The **Pride of Calais** *in 2003, the year before her bridge wings were totally enclosed thereby giving her navigating officers a greater degree of comfort during inclement weather. (John Hendy)*

*The second **Pride of Kent** was the former Zeebrugge freighter **European Highway**. She is seen leaving the Admiralty Pier extension shortly after her official naming ceremony in June 2003. (John Hendy)*

*The **Pride of Canterbury** was originally the freighter **European Pathway** and is seen arriving at Calais. The ship was off service throughout 2008 and early 2009 following an incident in The Downs, off Deal. (John Hendy)*

Farewell **Fantasia***! The* **PO Canterbury** *is seen leaving Calais on her last Saturday in service in May 2003. Her erstwhile sistership* **Fiesta** *(latterly* **SeaFrance Cezanne***) remained in service throughout 2008. (John Hendy)*

The 'Seaway' was sent to Falmouth to lay up and acted as a dormitory for the crews of her fleet companions during the annual round of refits. The freighter was put up for sale but she proved to be such a specialist ship that others who looked at her found her too expensive a vessel to convert to their own purposes. In June she sailed to Birkenhead and was removed from the sales list.

In late September 2004 it was announced that as from 3rd January 2005, the *European Seaway* would be reinstated while the *Pride of Burgundy* would return to passenger mode as from 10th January. Cuts were to be made elsewhere and the *Pride of Provence* was the next to go finishing on 20th December 2004. She became the third former P&O Ferries vessel to be sold to GA Ferries to whom she was handed over on 5th January, sailing to Greece a week later. She was renamed *Alkmini A* as had been the former *PO Canterbury*, and just like her she did not remain long in Greece being immediately chartered to Kystlink in May and becoming the *Pride of Telemark* when purchased in October 2005 and

used on the link between Langesund (Norway) and Hirtshals (Denmark). Following collision damage in the Danish port, she was later offered for sale.

The withdrawal of the *Pride of Aquitaine* followed. Her charter fees amounted to $20,750 a day (in excess of over £4 million a year) and so she was always an expensive ship to operate. In the circumstances it made little sense to continue running her and she duly finished on 16th May 2005. Quickly purchased by LD Lines, as the *Norman Spirit* she was used to reopen the Le Havre – Portsmouth link which P&O had previously closed. In July 2009, she is due to reopen the Dover - Boulogne service and will once again grace the Dover Strait.

The acquisition of the entire P&O Group by DP World in March 2006 left the ferry division in something of a quandary. DP World had purchased P&O for the vast assets in its ports portfolio but P&O Ferries was given an undertaking that there were no plans to sell off of what, after all, was only a very small part of the overall package. A major investment

The **Pride of Burgundy** *leaving Calais. (John Hendy)*

The second **European Endeavour** *was built as the* **Midnight Merchant** *and initially served on the Dover - Dunkirk West link. (John Hendy)*

this is my **P&O**

the UK's largest freight and passenger service

POferries.com
POferriesfreight.com

dover calais • **hull** zeebrugge / rotterdam • **portsmouth** bilbao • **teesport** zeebrugge / rotterdam
tilbury zeebrugge • **cairnryan / troon** larne • **liverpool** dublin

The roll on - roll off freighter **European Seaway** *maintains P&O Ferries' freight connection with Calais with the five dual-purpose vessels. (John Hendy)*

programme was promised and the first indication of some long-expected expansion came in spring 2007 with the purchase of the Spanish ro-pax vessel *El Greco*. Built as the *Midnight Merchant,* the ship was chartered by Norfolkline for its new Dover – Dunkirk West link and entered service in October 2000. She was eventually replaced by new purpose-built tonnage and left Dunkirk in August 2006 flying the Spanish flag for use on routes from Barcelona. P&O purchased the ship and she was renamed *European Endeavour* on 9th October, firstly operating from Liverpool to Dublin before an extended refit at Falmouth which included the unwelding of her bow door and the fitting of a 'cow-catcher' for use at Calais.

Although the 'Endeavour' is due to work as a relief on other P&O Ferries' routes in the North Sea, Irish Sea and between Dover and Calais, during summer 2008 she remained on the Dover Strait in order that P&O could continue to offer a six ship service following an unfortunate accident to the *Pride of Canterbury*.

This incident occurred on 31st January when during a period of foul weather when the port of Dover was closed to shipping, the ferry was sheltering in the Downs, off Deal. Whilst manoeuvring near the Goodwin Sands, her port screw made contact with a submerged wreck as a result of which the ferry was incapacitated and unable to operate normally. After a visit to Falmouth, she limped back to Dover on one screw and for several weeks operated in a freight mode during calm conditions. During

early June, it was eventually decided to mothball the ship at Dunkirk until full repairs, including the fitting of a new propeller shaft, could be carried out in November. The vessel was due to return to service before Christmas but further problems with her port gearbox prevented this.

After many years of speculation, during August 2008, P&O Ferries signed a Euro 360 million contract with Aker Yards in Ruama, Finland (later renamed STX Europe) for the two largest ferries ever to be constructed for the Dover-Calais service.

The first ship will enter service in December 2010 and the second in September 2011, replacing the *Pride of Dover* and the *Pride of Calais*.

At 49,000 gross tonnes and 210 metres in length, the two ferries will be the largest ships capable of fitting into existing facilities in the Channel ports and will be the first Channel ferries designed to manoeuvre under their own power in 50-knot winds.

Accommodation will be for more than 180 freight vehicles, more than doubling the freight carrying capacity of the ships they are replacing, whilst additionally providing a third vehicle deck for up to 195 tourist vehicles and up to 2,000 passengers.

Since 1980 P&O Ferries (and Townsend Thoresen before them) have led the way with the introduction of impressive new classes of Dover – Calais ferries and these new twins will surely become the leaders of an entire new generation of ship.

An artist's impression of the new 49,000 gross tons ships presently being built at STX Europe in Finland for the Dover - Calais route. They will replace the **Pride of Dover** *and* **Pride of Calais**. *(P&O Ferries)*

CHAPTER TEN

SEAFRANCE: THE FRENCH FERRY COMPANY

The cross-Channel fleet of French Railways (SNCF) had always played a secondary role to that of its British partners and throughout history, there were a number of occasions when the French Government appeared to be ready to rid itself of its subsidiary.

The last time that this occurred was during October 1987 when Sea Containers, owners of Sealink British Ferries, announced that it was planning to purchase SNCF Armement Naval should the French decide to rid themselves of their shipping division.

With SNCF heavily involved in the construction of the Channel Tunnel and TGV Nord, their ferry fleet represented a clash of interests. In typically forthright fashion, James Sherwood, for Sea Containers, announced that should the purchase come about then the *Cote d'Azur* and *Champs Elysees* would be stretched in line with the £5 million allocated to modify each of his two vessels, the *St. Anselm* and *St. Christopher*.

The purchase moved a little closer when during November 1988 it was announced in the shipping press that Sealink British Ferries were 'poised to take over the cross-Channel services of SNCF.' An agreement had been reached in principle under which Sealink British Ferries would be given the first option to purchase five French ships (two of which were based at Dieppe while a third operated the Dunkirk train ferry) in 1993. The French Government had still to give its approval but SNCF had reported that their initial reaction was favourable. However, the Transport

Minister had instructed SNCF to consult with the unions which represented the shipping division and therein lay an insurmountable obstacle. The story lost its interest and we must assume that French national pride combined with the weight of the unions knocked Sherwood's dream into touch.

In January 1990, the newly converted *Fiesta* (today the *SeaFrance Cezanne*) was transferred to the ownership of Societe Proprietaire des Navires (SPN), a new French independent subsidiary of SNCF in which Sealink British Ferries held a 49% share. This was due to the fact that funding for the purchase and the £12 million conversion of the *Fiesta* (then the freight ship *Channel Seaway*) and her sister ship *Fantasia* had been provided by Sealink UK Ltd and as Dover – Calais was a joint enterprise, the former ship was duly transferred to French operation. This was followed with the transfer of the second Calais-based ship, the *Cote d'Azur* to SPN ownership. The ownership of the UK-held 49% duly passed to the Swedish Stena Line when they acquired Sealink British Ferries in May 1990. In order to operate the French vessels, a further new company was founded – Societe Nouvelle d'Armement Transmanche, which was abbreviated to SNAT.

After Stena Line had taken over Sealink British Ferries in 1990, it was apparent that from the start that there existed a number of operational differences between them and their French partners. The Swedish-based company adopted a 'we know how to run ferries' approach which upset

*The 1974-built **Chartres** closed the Calais Maritime - Dover Admiralty Pier train-connected services in September 1993. She is seen leaving Calais in the livery of her charterers, the British-owned ALA company. (John Hendy)*

*The **SeaFrance Renoir** (ex **Cote d'Azur**) following modifications when her after bridge was replaced by a large extension to her self-service restaurant. The ship survived all her Sealink contemporaries and was in regular service during 2008. (John Hendy)*

*The **SeaFrance Manet** (ex **Champs Elysees**) was sent to Dieppe when replaced at Calais by the **Fiesta** but returned on the formation of SeaFrance. (John Hendy)*

*The **SeaFrance Monet** came to Calais from Dieppe where she had served as the **Versailles** and later the **Stena Londoner**. Hers was to be only the briefest association with the new French company. (John Hendy)*

*The train ferry **Nord Pas-de-Calais** was pressed into service on the Dover - Calais freight link until her new berth was ready at Dover. On the closure of the Dunkirk West train ferry service, she returned to Calais. The ship remains the most manoeuvrable of all local ferries. (John Hendy)*

Dover · SEAFRANCE · *Calais*

Cross Channel Excellence

With the arrival of the SeaFrance Molière in 2008, SeaFrance completed it's impressive fleet of new generation superferries operating the cross Channel route between Dover and Calais.

The SeaFrance Molière joined a distinguished fleet that includes the award winning SeaFrance Rodin and the SeaFrance Berlioz, both of which were custom built for the route. All three ships have capacity to effortlessly sail up to 1,900 passengers in style across the Channel.

Full specifications for each of the new generation superferries can be viewed by visiting seafrance.com, click the 'On board' tab then 'The Fleet' – Impressive indeed!

*The **SeaFrance Cezanne** (ex **Fiesta**) is seen off the South Foreland as she approaches Dover. (John Hendy)*

the French who rightly objected to being told to how to operate their own ships. Increasing changes and pressures were being forced upon them and when Stena took on the franchise of a well-known American fast food outlet and expected SNAT to follow suit, they declined to do so.

With the two companies growing further apart, it was hardly surprising that the five-year operating and trading agreement between Stena Sealink Line and Sealink SNAT ended on New Year's Day 1996 at which time the French announced that it would not be renewed and commenced independent operations as SeaFrance. In a company statement, M. Didier Bonnet (President of SNAT) said, 'After careful and exhaustive analysis of both companies' objectives and strategies, SNAT realised at the end of June 1995 that they were differing too widely and that it was not possible to come to a mutually satisfactory agreement'.

It is of interest that Sealink SNAT initially made advances to P&O European Ferries concerning a trading agreement but there were fears that should the Office of Fair Trading ever allow P&O and Stena to enter into a Joint Venture then the French position could be seriously weakened and the discussions came to nothing.

SeaFrance had originally stated that they were hoping to secure 12% of the market but some very aggressive undercutting of their competitors' rates saw 14.5% of passengers and 20% of the freight using their service within eighteen months.

Prior to the split, Stena Sealink had provided three ships for the Dover – Calais route: the *Stena Fantasia, Stena Invicta* and *Stena Challenger* while SNAT had supplied the *Fiesta* and *Cote d'Azur*. With the split in place, both concerns sought to enlarge their respective fleets both in order to compete with each other and also with P&O European Ferries.

Although she was then sixteen years old, the *Cote d'Azur* was sent to

ARNO at Dunkirk for a £5 million refit which included the addition of a large accommodation module at her after end in order to double the size of her self-service catering area. She returned to Calais as the *SeaFrance Renoir* while operating partner *Fiesta* became the *SeaFrance Cezanne*. They were assisted by the former train ferry *SeaFrance Nord Pas-de-Calais* which had closed the Dover – Dunkirk West route on 22nd December 1995 and which then took up a purely ro-ro role as from the following 7th January.

A third passenger ship was introduced on 3rd July in time for the 1996 summer schedules and was named *SeaFrance Monet* following a £500,000 refit prior to essential SOLAS modifications to keep her in service.

The ship had been built in Yugoslavia as the *Stena Nordica* in 1974 but was renamed *Stena Danica* before completion and operating the company's Gothenburg – Frederikshavn route until 1982 after which she was again named *Stena Nordica*. A further renaming to *Stena Nautica* then took place when she was chartered by RMT for three years to provide extra freight capacity on the Ostend – Dover link. The ship was subsequently purchased by SNCF for their Dieppe – Newhaven service where she operated as the *Versailles*. She was eventually chartered back to Stena when they took over the operation of the Dieppe link in May 1992 at which time she received the name *Stena Londoner*.

The *SeaFrance Monet's* period in service with SeaFrance was brief and she was eventually replaced by the *SeaFrance Manet* which, as the former *Champs Elysees*, had been replaced at Calais by the *Fiesta* in 1990. It will be remembered that she was moved to the Dieppe – Newhaven link and later renamed *Stena Parisien* when chartered by Stena Line in 1992. The ship was eventually handed back to her owners on 9th January 1997 and

The **SeaFrance Rodin** *was built at the Aker yard in Finland and is an excellent example of a twenty-first century cross-Channel ferry. Entering service in November 2001, she has quickly established herself as an efficient and comfortable vessel. (John Hendy)*

re-entered service eleven days later.

There followed a £1 million refit before the 'Manet' took up full service on 25th April replacing the *SeaFrance Monet* which went to lay-up at Dunkirk when it was expected that she would be sold for further trading. However, at the close of the year she was reactivated when the *SeaFrance Renoir* went off service requiring an emergency dry docking. Then during late May 1998, with the *SeaFrance Cezanne* experiencing mechanical problems, the 'Monet' once more returned to service and also deputised during the refit period in the following January.

At the end of the millennium, SeaFrance acquired the 49% which Stena Line had held in their ship-owning subsidiary SPN. It will be remembered that SPN had been created at the time when the *Fiesta* was passed to French control even though she was purchased and converted by Sealink British Ferries. The concern was latterly jointly owned by Sealink SNAT and Stena when they had operated the Dover – Calais service with the *Fiesta* and the *Cote d'Azur* but now Stena needed to raise money for their projected purchase of Scandlines. SeaFrance already 100% owned the 'Monet' and the 'Manet' which had both been Dieppe ships and the ro-ro vessel *Nord Pas-de-Calais* which had been based at Dunkirk.

The *SeaFrance Monet's* career came to an abrupt close during some particularly nasty weather on 29th March 2000. When approaching Calais in a NE gale, she hit the CA8 buoy and lost a stabiliser fin taking on huge amounts of water and arriving in port in a sinking condition. She was then blown heavily against berth 5 in gusts of up to 80 kph. The ship was promptly sent to Dunkirk and was sold on 18th May to Spanish owners Navieres Armas for service in the Canary Islands. As the *Volcan de Tacande*, she struck a rock on 30th January 2005 whilst on service

between Los Cristianos and La Gomera, was towed listing into port and later sold for scrapping.

NEW TONNAGE

Towards the close of 1999, SeaFrance were looking to purchase suitable second hand tonnage for the Calais – Dover route and showed particular interest in Irish Ferries' *Isle of Inishmore*. With that ship not available and all shipyard space in France occupied with new buildings, SeaFrance had no option but to order a new FF600 million super ferry from Aker Finnyards with an option to build a second.

The *SeaFrance Rodin* was the first purpose-built ferry for the route since 1992 and the first new French contribution to the service since that arrival of the *Champs Elysees* (*SeaFrance Manet*) in 1984. The ship entered service on 29th November 2001 and was described as 'a French Masterpiece' by the public relations officials. At 34,000 gross tons, the futuristically designed ferry measured 185 metres by 27.7 metres and was capable of accommodating 2,000 lane metres of freight (120 lorries or 700 cars) and 1,900 passengers. Her most abiding feature is undoubtedly the starboard side atrium which brings a cruise-ship experience to a cross-Channel ferry.

It was originally envisaged that the new ship would replace the *SeaFrance Renoir* but with SeaFrance in an expansionist mood, she was retained in the fleet where she continued to play a full and important part.

Riding on the wave of success provided by the 'Rodin,' on 24th June 2003 came the order for a sister ship to be built at Chantiers de l'Atlantique at St. Nazaire and her keel was duly laid on 22nd October. As the *SeaFrance Berlioz*, the ship finally entered service on 4th April

The ferry with the longest name ever to serve on the Dover - Calais route is undoubtedly the **SeaFrance Nord Pas-de-Calais**. *Here she is in her freight role approaching Calais in 2008.* (John Hendy)

Following the success of the **SeaFrance Rodin**, *a sister ship appeared in April 2005 allowing the company to operate a fleet of six ships. Built at St Nazaire, the* **SeaFrance Berlioz** *is seen leaving Dover in September 2008.* (John Hendy)

Rather than build a third 'Rodin' class ferry, SeaFrance purchased the sale-listed overnight ferry **Jean Nicoli** *(ex* **Superfast X**). *After a protracted conversion for day usage, the* **SeaFrance Moliere** *finally entered full service in October 2008. Her narrow beam can be appreciated in this view. (John Hendy)*

2005 and after experimenting with crew arrangements, SeaFrance were able to offer a six-ship service although there was never an occasion when all six vessels were operational at the same time.

The design of the 'Berlioz' closely follows that of the 'Rodin' although her interior is brighter and less restrained with much use of lime greens, oranges and r..eds. Without doubt, both sisters are extremely comfortable and attractive vessels and, both in looks and interior design, have certainly set the trend for the new millennium.

By spring 2007, SeaFrance were looking to build both a third 'Rodin' class ferry in addition to a new ro-ro freighter to replace the *SeaFrance Nord Pas-de-Calais*. In the event, matters were to take a completely different and more immediate course.

On 28th December 2007, SeaFrance announced that they had purchased the *Jean Nicoli* (ex *Superfast X*) for Euro 105 million from Mediterranean operators SNCM. The 30,441 gross ton ship was built in Germany and entered service in May 2002 on her owners' North Sea link between Rosyth and Zeebrugge.

In August 2006, the *Superfast X* was acquired by Veolia Transport (SNCM) for Euro 112 million in order to assist in their bid for the Marseilles – Corsica contract but was almost immediately offered for resale. A summer charter to Crete operators ANEK was hastily arranged before the ship was laid up in Marseilles.

Capable of speeds up to 28 knots – which she will never require in her new role - the 203 metre long ship's capacity was for 730 passengers and 660 cars. Being an overnight ship, much of her accommodation was composed of cabins which needed stripping out for her short-sea work between Calais and Dover.

SeaFrance took her over in early April 2008 and sailed her to ARNO at Dunkirk for a projected Euro 15 million conversion (actually Euro 20 million) to a high capacity day ferry capable of carrying 1,200 passengers. Renamed *SeaFrance Moliere*, the vessel was due in service on 1st July

although delays in finishing her off saw this delayed until later in the autumn. The ship eventually took up service in a freight mode on 19th August and, after several false starts, commenced full service on 1st October.

The arrival of the new vessel inevitably saw the end of the earlier generation *SeaFrance Manet* which was withdrawn on 29th April, immediately after the 'Rodin' had reappeared from a two-month refit at Dunkirk. The 'Manet' had been operating on a thrice-daily basis and in a freight capacity for some time but with the 20.15 from Calais and the 21.35 return, the ship was finally laid up leaving the *SeaFrance Renoir* to run the same schedules until she in turn finished on 25th July. However, SeaFrance decided to retain her as a relief vessel and this decision was fully justified when during September, the Channel Tunnel experienced its second major fire and the ports of Dover and Calais both made hay in what would have otherwise been a quiet third quarter of the year.

With the full entry into service of the new 'Moliere,' the *SeaFrance Cezanne* was downgraded and adopted the role of freight ship with a reduced passenger certificate for 250.

Following significant financial losses during the period 2007 - 2008, in January 2009 SeaFrance held crisis talks with its parent company SNCF at which initial plans to reduce both the size of the workforce and fleet numbers were discussed. This was unacceptable to SNCF and a further month was given in order for SeaFrance to review the company's future. At a meeting during February, a loss of 650 jobs and a future three ship fleet was agreed upon. The *SeaFrance Cezanne* finished service on 13th February after which she went to lay up at Dunkirk but the *SeaFrance Renoir* was retained to cover the period of refits. The company hopes to return to profitability in 2010.

During its brief existence, SeaFrance has established itself as a major player in the cross-Channel market.

CHAPTER ELEVEN

HOVERSPEED: DECLINE AND FALL

The Hoverspeed story is one of what might have been had funds been available to expand and develop the hovercraft concept. Sadly, it was not to be and the 'wave piercing' catamarans, which eventually replaced them, failed to make the same impact or capture the public's imagination. They were between 15 – 30 minutes faster on the crossing than the conventional ferries but did not save enough time to make a huge amount of difference on projected journey times to chosen Continental destinations. Neither did they offer much in the way of on board facilities when compared with the vessels with which they were competing. Whereas the hovercraft were always perceived as an exciting innovation, the catamarans were simply small ferries.

EARLY HOVERCRAFT

The research vessel SNR1 crossed the Dover Strait between Calais and Dover in 2 hours on 25th July 1959 with Sir Christopher Cockerell (its inventor) on board. However, there was still much to do before the cushion craft could commence a commercial service although during the early 1960s, pleasure flights were operated from the Wirral across the Dee estuary to Rhyl in north Wales, from Eastney (near Portsmouth) to Ryde on the Isle of Wight and in the Bristol Channel.

Commercial services across the English Channel did not start until 1966 when the Swedish company Hoverlloyd introduced twin 36-seater SRN6 ('Winchester' class) craft on their Ramsgate to Calais service. At Dover, Townsend Car Ferries soon followed with a similar craft named *Britannia* although inclement weather and technical problems saw her services prematurely end after little more than a month.

The first Hoverport at Calais opened on 30th April 1966 and was situated in a restricted area immediately inside the West Pier.

The first £1.75 million car carrying 'Mountbatten' class hovercraft was launched at the East Cowes yard of the British Hovercraft Corporation in February 1968 and, as the *Princess Margaret*, made her maiden flight between Dover and Boulogne on 11th June for the British Rail hovercraft subsidiary, Seaspeed. She was followed in December by Hoverlloyd's first SRN4, named *Swift*, while in the following June she was joined by a second craft, *Sure*. Seaspeed's *The Princess Anne*, commenced operations at Dover in August 1969.

At Calais, the new Hoverport was opened in the dunes to the east of the port on 26th June 1969.

Such was the initial popularity and success of the new service that Hoverlloyd introduced the *Sir Christopher* in June 1972 and later

This view of the Calais hoverport shows all three types of cross-Channel hovercraft on the pad. On the left is SNCF's unsuccessful double-decked SEDAM N500 **Ingenieur Jean-Bertin**, *in the centre an SRN 4 Mk III and on the right an SRN 4 Mk II. (Calais Chamber of Commerce)*

The Mk III hovercraft **The Princess Margaret** *raises her skirt on the River Thames shortly after her conversion in May 1979. (Westland Aerospace)*

The Princess Anne *arriving at Dover's hoverport on her final day of operation on 1st October 2000. (John Hendy)*

The **SeaCat Danmark** *in her Hoverspeed livery. (John Hendy)*

The **SeaCat Scotland** *advertising that she is a SeaCat, arriving off Calais in May 2003. (John Hendy)*

*On board **The Princess Anne** for an 08.00 flight to Calais in August 2000. The small cockpit very much resembles that of an aeroplane. (John Hendy)*

converted all three Ramsgate-based craft to Mark II specification increasing their capacity from 250 to 288 passengers and from 30 to 37 cars. A fourth craft, the *Prince of Wales*, joined the Ramsgate fleet during June 1977 and was built as a Mark II.

Seaspeed responded by stretching their twin craft by 55 ft to Mark III status allowing them to carry 396 passengers and 55 cars. The increased size of the stretched craft saw the original pad at the Eastern Docks closed in favour of a new £14 million hoverport at the Western Docks, situated between the Prince of Wales' Pier and the North Pier, which opened in July 1978.

Merger talks between Hoverlloyd and Seaspeed had been taking place for a number of years and the 'go ahead' was finally given during summer 1981; the new company was to be known as Hoverspeed. In the following year, the Ramsgate (Pegwell Bay) operations were closed and all services were concentrated on Dover. The unsuccessful French SEDAM N500 hovercraft *Ingenieur Jean-Bertin* was briefly taken into the new company fleet in 1983 but after four months was returned to SNCF as being unsuitable. The same year saw the *Sure* laid up at Pegwell Bay and used for 'spares' for the remainder of the fleet.

In 1984 Hoverspeed was sold to its directors for a nominal sum after which a £3.2 million loss was turned into a £194,000 pre-tax profit within two years. Then in 1986, the company was again sold for £5 million to Sea Containers of Bermuda whose President, James Sherwood, announced that he was not hopeful that the hovercraft fleet would continue in service. As we have seen, Sea Containers had lost control of Sealink British Ferries in 1990 and at the close of the 1991 season, the three former Ramsgate craft were withdrawn from service in favour of the new generation of SeaCats which it was stated would be the answer to the Channel Tunnel.

SEACAT REVOLUTION

Sherwood announced that his new fleet of five SeaCats would revolutionise the whole of the European ferry industry by splitting it in two – catamarans for passengers and their cars and conventional ferries for freight. Construction of the first of the 74-metre craft commenced at the InCat yard in Hobart, Tasmania and the first was the *Hoverspeed Great Britain*. Features provided in their passenger areas included a panoramic view of the sea from the main central and side lounges, with every passenger having a comfortable, aircraft-style seat. The Observation Deck allowed passengers a view forward through the Flight Deck (or bridge control area) while at the after end, a lounge bar served drinks and light refreshments.

After her launch in January 1990, the 'HGB' crossed the Pacific Ocean and claimed the fabled Hales Trophy for the Blue Riband of the Atlantic which she crossed in 3 days, 7 hours 54 minutes. She arrived in the UK on a wave of unprecedented media coverage before commencing a problem-ridden first season on the Portsmouth – Cherbourg link. After a 'show the flag' visit to the Isle of Man, the 'HGB' arrived at Dover on 20th November where crossings to Boulogne and Calais were made before she headed for the Pool of London where the Hales Trophy was formally presented.

A final crossing between Portsmouth and Cherbourg was made on 6th January 1991 before Hoverspeed announced that the 74 metre craft would be better used on services from Dover. The *Hoverspeed France* had been launched in April 1990 while the *SeaCat Tasmania* followed during October. The fourth SeaCat was named *Hoverspeed Belgium* in January 1991. The hovercraft meanwhile received new liveries to match those of the SeaCats while their passenger spaces were reduced from 425 to 300.

The *Hoverspeed France* took up service from Dover to Boulogne on 1st July 1991 while the 'HGB' started operating to Calais on 20th July. At the end of that year, Stena Line withdrew from the historic Folkestone – Boulogne link leaving a considerable gap in the cross-Channel market and the newly built *Hoverspeed Boulogne* (launched as *Hoverspeed Belgium*) was earmarked to reopen the link which she duly did on 11th April 1992. She was a great improvement on the earlier SeaCats with much seating grouped around tables rather than in simple aircraft-style fashion and was also fitted with a ride control system which the 'HGB' had received during March 1992.

Meanwhile the fifth SeaCat was named *SeaCat Scotland* and arrived in the UK at the end of March 1992. She initially operated from Dover to cover overhauls and to allow the *Hoverspeed France* to have her ride control system fitted before commencing a new Irish Sea link between Stranraer and Belfast. The Australian-based *SeaCat Tasmania* was then used to operate the summer Dover – Calais route with the two remaining hovercraft while the *Hoverspeed France* was renamed *Sardegna Express* for a bareboat charter in the Mediterranean. Her return in December 1992 was premature due to the non-payment of charter fees and should have seen her on the Holyhead – Dublin route but problems with berthing rights saw her earmarked instead for a new route linking Gothenburg and Frederikshavn.

In the event, she was placed on the Folkestone – Boulogne link and renamed *SeaCat Boulogne* while the *Hoverspeed Boulogne* sailed to the

*The **Swift** approaching Dover hoverport on an afternoon service from Calais during September 1991. (John Hendy)*

Following the withdrawal of the hovercraft in 2000, the Italian-built **SuperSeaCat One** *appeared at Dover with two of her sisters for the following season. (John Hendy)*

The **SuperSeaCat Two** *came to Dover directly from her builders in 1997 but only lasted until the end of the season. Here she is in the Pool of London in June that year. (Hoverspeed)*

The **SuperSeaCat France** was never to operate for Sea Containers and was the subject of a 'contractual disagreement' with her builders in 1995. (Hoverspeed)

The **Atlantic II** (ex **SeaCat Tasmania**) arriving at Calais in August 1999. (John Hendy)

Kattegat as the *SeaCatamaran Danmark* in competition with the established Stena Line service. There was never any love lost between Sea Containers and Stena and the strategy behind the operation of this new service may have been rather more than for commercial reasons.

Meanwhile the *SeaCat Tasmania* had finished service at the close of September having worked the season without a marine escape system which prevented her from operating in seas above 2.5 metre wave height – a whole metre less than her fleet companions.

After a surprise winter charter to Ferrylineas running across the River Plate in South America, the 'HGB' was sent to assist the *SeaCat Scotland* in the North Channel during summer 1992. Later in the year, Hoverspeed were forced to bring back *The Princess Anne* into winter operation as there was no spare SeaCat available. Then, following the closure of the Tasmanian service, the *SeaCat Tasmania* was again brought back from Australia to support the Dover – Calais schedules. It was initially planned to send her to run on the Vancouver – Seattle route but exorbitant port charges saw her come back to the UK. Prior to her arrival, the linkspan used by Hoverspeed's SeaCats at the Eastern Docks was moved and reconstructed at the Western Docks, adjacent to the hoverpad and the Prince of Wales' Pier, thus allowing all operations to be handled at the International Hoverport.

During the summer of 1993, the twin Mark III hovercraft were once again the mainstay of the Dover – Calais route, operating with the *SeaCat Tasmania* which was given full Hoverspeed livery. The SeaCats seemed to enjoy a butterfly existence as no sooner had they established themselves in any particular port, they were off somewhere else without ever being given the chance to consolidate their service. The only exception to this was the *SeaCat Scotland* which remained in the North Channel for the majority of her career with Sea Containers.

The reserve hovercraft *Prince of Wales* caught fire on the pad at Dover during early April 1993 and her port cabin was destroyed. She was later broken up. During July the *SeaCat Tasmania* was named *SeaCat Calais* and operated with the *SeaCat Boulogne*, alternating on both the Dover and Folkestone stations. However, SeaCat services were temporarily suspended in November when the hovercraft maintained the Calais service. Following the 'HGB's' winter charter to Ferrylineas, the *SeaCat Calais* was now chartered for the River Plate service for a period of five years and was subsequently renamed *Atlantic II*.

The year 1994 saw the *SeaCat Boulogne* transferred to the Isle of Man services from mid-June (becoming the *SeaCat Isle of Man*) while the 'HGB' had her passenger certificate raised from 450 to 600 in order to cope with the increasing number of day-trippers on the Folkestone – Boulogne link. Only one SeaCat was thus available to Hoverspeed during the summer months and once again, the company strategy was called into question; to remove the SeaCat fleet from the centre of their operations and leave their premier route in the hands of two venerable hovercraft seemed a strange move for a go-ahead company. However, as Hoverspeed chartered the craft from parent company Sea Containers at high rates, it may have been a safer move to sub-charter them at a guaranteed fixed price rather than risk them making a loss on the company's home routes. It was all rather different from 1991 when it had been announced that four SeaCats were the future of the Dover and Folkestone stations.

With the introduction of the SeaCat fleet, Sea Containers had certainly taken the ferry world by storm and now others wished to emulate their success. Sherwood believed that his company had held a commercial protection agreement with InCat. However, when two further craft were sold to South American owners who quickly passed them on to bitter rivals Stena Sealink Line for operation in the Irish Sea, Sherwood showed his irritation by looking elsewhere before ordering the first of the second-generation craft.

During early May 1994, a SuperSeaCat was ordered from Austal Ships of Western Australia. The design was for a craft which was 5 metres longer than InCat's 74-metre SeaCats but which would accommodate 184 cars (more than double the number) and 600 passengers. Sherwood announced that the new craft would replace the SeaCats which were now 'capacity constrained' and would in future be used on start-up routes. He also stated that the new craft would not be built by InCat because of 'technical problems' with the earlier 74-metre vessels.

In the event, 'contractual difficulties' caused Austal Ships not to release the *SuperSeaCat France* for the summer 1995 season although Sea Containers claimed that they had rejected the craft as her trial speed fell well below the minimum contract requirement. The unfortunate vessel was eventually acquired for use in the Kattegat and then the Baltic and today links Algeciras with Tangiers as the *Alcantara Dos*.

The SRN4 *Swift* was towed to Gosport in June 1994 to be the main attraction at the nearby Hovercraft Museum. The £2 million craft was donated by Hoverspeed but was later broken up.

A memorandum from Hoverspeed's Managing Director to his staff during late September outlined 'The Way Forward' with the announcement that the Folkestone – Boulogne SeaCat service was to become seasonal.

Nevertheless, this retrenchment did not prevent a new livery

This May 2003 Calais view shows the arrival of the 74-metre craft **Hoverspeed Great Britain** *and the departure of the* **SeaCat Scotland**. *(John Hendy)*

appearing for the 1995 season when SeaCat funnels and hovercraft fins became a red with the catamarans receiving blue hulls. The SeaCats had the word 'SeaCat' applied to their superstructures while the hovercraft received the word 'Hovercraft' on their bow and stern doors.

The *SeaCat Isle of Man* was back on the Dover – Calais link in January 1995 before being renamed *SeaCat Norge* in 1996 for service in the Kattegat on a new SeaCo – Color Line partnership while on 14th September 1996 *The Princess Anne* made a record crossing of the Dover Strait in just 22 minutes.

Record carryings were reported on both Dover Strait crossings in 1996 while on the Dover – Calais crossing, the *SeaCat Norge* appeared with the *SeaCat Danmark* during November, both in the livery of Color Line to whom they had been on charter.

The last day of February 1997 witnessed the closure of the historic UK – Ostend ferry service which had been operated by the Belgian Government since 1846. For its last few years, the link had operated from Ramsgate in conjunction with Sally Ferries and on the following day, a new service commenced using a pair of InCat 81-metre catamarans named *Holyman Diamant* and *Holyman Rapide*. The new operators were the Australian company Holyman who briefly flourished before discovering precisely why the Belgians had found it so difficult to operate profitably on this secondary route.

During spring 1997, Sea Containers Ferries reflagged its four 74-metre SeaCats in the UK with the *Hoverspeed Great Britain* being registered at Folkestone, the *SeaCat Danmark* and *SeaCat Norge* at Newhaven and the *SeaCat Scotland* at Stranraer. The *SeaCat Norge* was again named *SeaCat Isle of Man* and after a March refit took up the Dover – Calais service with the twin hovercraft. In her earlier guises as the

SeaCat Boulogne and *Hoverspeed France* the craft had previously served in the Dover Strait. However, the SeaCat was replaced in June after the arrival of the £22 million Fincantieri-built monohull *SuperSeaCat Two* directly from her Italian builders. With capacity for 774 passengers and 175 cars the new craft firstly showed herself in the Pool of London before commencing service on 25th June.

At the end of the year, the *SuperSeaCat Two* left Dover on 18th December bound for a Falmouth refit before being switched to the Liverpool – Dublin link while the *SeaCat Isle of Man* again took up station at Dover on the following day. Hers was to be a familiar presence until in April 1999 she was moved to the Irish Sea in place of the *SuperSeaCat Two* which was transferred to Newhaven – Dieppe. Both SRN4 hovercraft were refurbished 'in house' during spring 1999 when the company welcomed back the *Atlantic II* (ex *SeaCat Tasmania*, ex *SeaCat Calais*) after a five-year stint operating across the River Plate. She began service on 30th April but the ending of duty-free concessions two months later was to hit the company hard.

In March 1998 the Ostend – Dover link was reintroduced when Holyman – Sally's Ramsgate service was switched back to its historic UK home in a Hoverspeed-Holyman joint venture.

During autumn 1999, the 81-metre former Ostend craft *Rapide* was engaged on the Calais service operating four trips each day while both hovercraft were on overhaul. The work centred on their port sides which were both upgraded to First Class standards, thereby giving a higher quality of service for the fewer number of passengers anticipated since the demise of duty-free. In the same year, Hoverspeed purchased the remaining 50% of the Ostend business from the Ramsgate – Ostend operators Holyman which included the *Rapide* and *Diamant*.

The 81-metre **SeaCat Diamant** *originally served the Ramsgate (and later Dover) - Ostend service. Both she and her sister* **Rapide** *received this livery in 2004. Eventually receiving the 'SeaCat' prefix, they closed the Hoverspeed service in November 2005. (John Hendy)*

FINALE

On 1st October 2000, the twin SRN4 hovercraft, *The Princess Margaret* and *The Princess Anne* were finally withdrawn from service and somehow the heart of Hoverspeed died with them. To many, they were the craft around which Hoverspeed's niche market was built. Yes they were old, they were noisy, they shook even in the calmest weather, they were capacity constrained and with the cost of aviation fuel rising to unprecedented heights, they were expensive to run and maintain. Yet they were a uniquely British invention and many mourned their passing. *The Princess Anne* ran her final flight at 17.00 from Dover with *The Princess Margaret* bringing down the curtain an hour later.

Then there was a staff special operated by *The Princess Anne* which left Dover at 19.15. Arriving back at 20.30, the craft crept up onto the beach in front of the old White Cliffs Hotel where a farewell party was in full swing.

On the same day, the Sea Containers subsidiary closed the Folkestone – Boulogne route forever and the *Hoverspeed Great Britain* was thereby freed to operate the new catamaran service to Calais on the following day in tandem with the *SeaCat Danmark*.

The twin SRN4s were eventually taken to the Hovercraft Museum at Lee on the Solent and were duly offered for sale.

Perhaps in order to temper any backlash that the Sea Containers management perceived might possibly occur as a result of the unpopular withdrawal of the SRN4 hovercraft, the 2001 season surprisingly saw three of the four 'SuperSeaCats' based at Dover – two on the Calais service with the other running to Ostend. Yet previous experience with the *SuperSeaCat Two* had shown that these stern loaders were far from the ideal craft for the high-density, quick turn round link and schedules suffered as a result of their operation. Without doubt, by far the most successful SeaCats were the 74-metre variety which allowed simple and slick drive-through operation and fast turn rounds. At the end of the

2001 season it was all change yet again.

After the Ostend link had been axed in December 2002, the Dover – Calais route became seasonal when Hoverspeed closed their Dover – Calais service between December 2003 and March 2004 after which the *SeaCat Scotland* was introduced. Another livery change occurred when the 81-metre craft both reappeared with huge union flags along their hulls and superstructures while the *SeaCat France* (ex *Atlantic II*) received an expensive overhaul and became the third craft for the summer season operating briefly with the *Rapide* and *Diamant* between 17th July and 31st August only.

Then the Newhaven – Dieppe route was closed in 2004 after failing to reopen for its summer service in April. The seasonal Calais link again restarted on 17th March 2005 but the writing had long been on the wall. The twin 81-metre craft operated together throughout the final season which was due to finish on 23rd December. However, the *SeaCat Diamant* finally closed the service on 7th November with the company claiming that it was simply unable to sustain its losses.

It had all been a long and protracted fall from grace which was not entirely due to market forces, the rising price of fuel or even the ending of duty-free concessions. There were so many expensive changes of name and unnecessary switches of craft with so many numerous possibilities presenting themselves for redeployment that few routes could ever have known in advance what they might be operating during the following season. Apart from the twin hovercraft, there was never any impression of permanence – the management's policy appeared to be one of short-termism and a lasting feature of the manner in which the company was operated concerned its sudden and often surprise changes of strategy. In addition to this, the constant and costly livery changes may have looked very pretty but certainly failed to generate any much-needed traffic for the ailing company.

CHAPTER TWELVE

HARBOURS & RAILWAYS: THE CHANGING SCENE

DOVER

It has been seen how the development of the vehicle industry has demanded a complete reappraisal of both port and port approach infrastructure. At Dover, the emphasis was for so long on the train-connected services from the Admiralty Pier at the western end of the harbour. Passengers would board the Continental Boat Express at London's Charing Cross and Cannon Street stations (before 1914) and latterly at Victoria, and be transported to the quayside at Dover where their luggage, along with assorted mailbags, was hoisted aboard the waiting steamer.

The interchange was simple and trouble free; it was a tried and tested system made possible because the railway companies operated both the trains and the ships. The cross-Channel steamer was an extension of the railway system and its operation fitted the finely honed railway timetables of Britain and Continental Europe. Rough weather in the Dover Strait might cause a delayed arrival and missed connections that might cause serious 'knock-on' effects from Calais to Brindisi or Constantinople. In view of this, it was therefore important to build a certain degree of reserve power into any new cross-Channel steamer and they were all noted for their ease of handling in confined spaces, their acceleration away from

harbours, their speed in coming astern using the bow-rudder and the excellent seamanship of their officers and crews.

The South Eastern Railway built their main line from London (London Bridge) by way of Reigate, Tonbridge, Ashford to Folkestone which was reached in June 1843. The construction of the line had been fairly straight forward but having reached Folkestone, the 19 arches of the Foord viaduct required over a million bricks to complete before the Victorian engineers were faced with an area known as the Warren. This is the coastal area between Folkestone and Dover which lies on a landslip with the sea on one side and the base of the cliffs on the other. It is composed of soft gault clay and the weight and pressure of the saturated chalk cliffs on the soft and slippery clay beneath it continues to be a great concern for today's engineers. It is a geologically unstable area and in addition three long tunnels through the chalk were necessary before the railway reached Dover. This was finally achieved on 7th February 1844 when the new terminus at the base of the Admiralty Pier was reached by burrowing under Archcliffe Fort; 87.75 miles from London.

In September 1853, the four-storeyed Italianate-style Lord Warden Hotel was opened for business adjacent to the Admiralty Pier as 'the best place at which to break the journey to or from the Continent.' During

The romance of steam is beautifully captured in this Edwardian post card of a Continental Boat Express led by a Wainwright D Class 4-4-0 at speed exiting Shakespeare Tunnel on its way to the Admiralty Pier. (John Hendy collection)

The British Railways' Standard Class 'Pacific' 'William Shakespeare' hauling a down 'Golden Arrow' express in the late 'fifties. A new rake of Pullman cars was supplied in 1951. (John Hendy collection)

With the original Admiralty Pier station on the extreme right, this image shows the infilling for the new Marine Station in about 1909. A Belgian mail steamer and one of the 1898 Nord paddlers lie on the extension. (John Hendy collection)

How cargo used to be carried. The SE&CR vessel **Maidstone** of 1899 is busy discharging at Calais. (John Hendy collection)

The twin-hulled **Calais-Douvres** at the outside berth on the Admiralty Pier in about 1885. The South Eastern's railway lines to the right led to Charing Cross while the left hand tracks took London Chatham & Dover Railway trains to Victoria. (John Hendy collection)

periods of inclement weather, many people would prefer to wait there rather than risk a Channel crossing on which they might become ill. After many years as Southern House, the home to the local railway shipping division, this splendid edifice continues to grace the wasteland of this most forgotten area of the town as Lord Warden House.

Railway Mania was then gripping the country and there were many instances of rival railway companies attempting to capture traffic from areas of the United Kingdom which were quite unable to withstand the pressures of competition and all that this involved. Some of the bitterest competition took place in Kent with the arrival in Dover of the grandly named London Chatham & Dover Railway on 22nd July 1861. Unlike its bitter rival's line, the LC&DR's tracks crossed the North Downs and presented a far greater challenge to its engineers. From London, the line climbed up and over the Downs and into the Medway and Stour valleys at Rochester and Canterbury before reaching Dover – a distance of 78 miles. Approaching Dover from Canterbury, the line plunged into two tunnels before arriving at Dover Town. Just three months later, it pushed on through a further tunnel to Dover Harbour station which was situated alongside the Basin (after 1874 the Granville Dock). This station was intended to handle all the main passenger traffic and in order to show that this was indeed so, the Town station was renamed Dover Priory in July 1863 thereby removing the principal title in favour of one which pointed to the nearby St Martin's Priory. The 'Harbour' station still exists as a store although it was closed in 1927. The South Eastern Railway did not take long before they adopted the 'Town' suffix for their original

station adjacent to the Admiralty Pier, even though it was some way from what it claimed to be.

In 1864, the Chatham Company pushed on past the Lord Warden Hotel and on to the Admiralty Pier, three years after the South Eastern had established itself there. It became a favourite occupation of Dovorians to stand in Lord Warden Square to watch and take daily wagers upon which of the rivals' Boat Expresses, coming from totally different directions, would first run onto the Admiralty Pier.

Thus, from 1864 all Continental Boat Expresses used the confined Dover Admiralty Pier station where there was only room for a double line and two extremely narrow platforms. In those days, ships berthed either side of the pier and doors on the outward side allowed passengers access to the trains. However, with a brisk south-westerly wind blowing up Channel, waves frequently broke over the pier making the movement of passengers and their luggage extremely difficult and unpleasant not to say dangerous. As traffic volumes increased, something better was required.

In 1909, work started on reclaiming an area immediately to the east of the original Admiralty Pier in order to lay the foundations for a new Marine Station. As can be seen in the illustrations, much infilling was required before work on the actual station building could commence in 1913 but its completion occurred during the First World War and it was eventually opened for military use in February 1915.

Instead of handling the Continental travellers for which it was designed, soldiers and military equipment passed through the station on their way to the Somme and Flanders while sick and wounded returned

Calais Maritime station in the 1930s with the **Canterbury** alongside and a Nord 'Pacific' class locomotive ready to leave with the 'Fleche d'Or'. (John Hendy collection)

The Merchant Navy class 'Pacific' 'French Line CGT' about to enter Shakespeare Tunnel with the President of France on a State Visit during March 1950. (John Hendy collection)

*Calais Maritime in about 1900 with the paddle steamer **Dover** alongside. (John Hendy collection)*

*A good view of Dover's Western Docks in about 1955 with the Admiralty Pier and Marine Station to the right of the three ships. The **Invicta** separates the Belgian vessels **Prince Baudouin** (forward) and one of the two **Koning Albert** class (astern). The Prince of Wales' Pier is on the left as is the area, at its shoreward end, later occupied by the hoverport. (FotoFlite)*

*Dover Harbour from the west in about 1959 showing the Admiralty Pier berths with (l to r) the **Reine Astrid**, **Invicta**, **Roi Leopold III** and the **Isle of Thanet**. The **Saint-Germain** is in the train ferry dock while the Eastern Docks Car Ferry Terminal is occupied by the **Lord Warden** and **Artevelde**. (FotoFlite)*

with those on leave. With its strong connection with the war to end all wars, it was indeed fitting that the South Eastern & Chatham Railway's impressive war memorial was sited at the station in 1922. The building was opened for civilian use on 18th January 1919 and with due pomp and ceremony, in November 1920 the body of the Unknown Warrior was landed from the destroyer HMS *Verdun* before being taken to Westminster Abbey in London.

The most famous train to use the 'Marine' was undoubtedly the 'Golden Arrow' which operated from May 1929 until its demise in September 1972, although by the end it was but a shadow of its former self.

The French had introduced the 'Fleche d'Or' all-Pullman train linking Paris with Calais in 1926 and the Southern Railway followed suite, building the *Canterbury* to carry the 300 First Class passengers across the Dover Strait. On the launch of the new service, trains left Victoria and the Gare du Nord at 11.00 daily and the ten-coach 'Arrow' was usually hauled by one of Maunsell's impressive 4-6-0 'Lord Nelson' class locos which took 98 minutes for their sprint through Kent.

After the war, the 'Arrow' was re-winged in April 1946 and in 1951 a new set of Pullman cars was introduced. Bullied's 'Merchant Navy,' 'West Country' or 'Battle of Britain' 4-6-2 Pacific class locomotives now hauled the train while towards the end of steam, two new BR 4-6-2 'Britannia' Standard class Pacifics ('William Shakespeare' or 'Oliver Cromwell') were also used. In October 1952, the 'Arrow' was retimed and used the Folkestone – Calais route on its outward run but in May 1960, it reverted to Dover.

Steam gave way to electric traction when the South Eastern main line was electrified in 1961 after which Class 71 locomotives took over the

running of the fabled train until its inevitable withdrawal at the end of September 1972. Some of the 'Golden Arrow' Pullman cars still exist and work on the 'Orient Express' while others have passed into the hands of preservation societies.

With the delayed opening of the Channel Tunnel, the through services linking Paris (Gare du Nord) to Calais Maritime and London (Victoria) to Dover Western Docks, ended with the final sailing of the *Chartres* on 24th September 1993. Although the Ostend jetfoils continued to run until the end of the year, the old Dover Marine station closed for business exactly twelve months later (24th September 1994) although there was a special steam hauled train operated on the following day. Unadvertised passenger trains continued using the station until November 1994 but the rail connection was severed in 1996.

Today, the 'Marine' station is part of Dover's Cruise Terminal and is a listed building, ensuring its future as an important part of Dover's maritime and railway history.

Hand in hand with the development of the ferry industry at both Dover and Calais has been the advances in port infrastructure to accommodate the huge ferries that today work non-stop across the Dover Strait.

The advent of the car ferry era initially saw the lift on – lift off method being used but side loading drive on – drive off was introduced in 1936 when the Dunkirk train ferry commenced operations. Each of the three steamers had small garages at the after end of their Boat Decks allowing some 25 cars to be stowed.

Traffic growth saw Dover Harbour Board build their Eastern Docks Car Ferry Terminal which opened for business on 30th June 1953 and has never looked back. Although ever since their start in 1928, Townsend

*This 1965 view of the Eastern Docks Car Ferry Terminal shows the **Lord Warden** in berth 2 and berth 4 under construction. The port's first double-decked linkspan lies in the car park ready to be jacked into position. (John Hendy)*

*Calais Maritime and harbour in 1982 with Sealink's **Cote d'Azur** and **St Christopher** in berths 4 and 3. All this infrastructure has been removed and the present berths lie in the new harbour at the top of the picture. (Calais Chamber of Commerce)*

Bros Car Ferries had always operated from the Camber at the Eastern Docks, the opening of the Car Ferry Terminal began a complete re-emphasis and readjustment of traffic using the port. As post-war social trends changed, gradually and inevitably, fewer people travelled to the Continent by train and ship, preferring instead to use the flexibility of their family cars.

With the Eastern Docks now capacity constrained and with little space for future expansion, Dover Harbour Board have published plans costing £420 million to redevelop the Western Docks with the construction of their Terminal 2. This far-reaching scheme sweeps away even more of the historic old port of Dover by infilling the Granville Dock and Tidal Harbour and linking the Wellington Dock directly with the harbour by way of a new lock across the Marine Parade. The area of reclamation also includes the former hoverport and the loss to public use of one of the town's greatest assets, the Prince of Wales' Pier, which will be shortened by 80 metres. Three new linkspans (berths 10, 11 and 12) will be created to the east of the pier with a further berth (number 14) on the west while on the eastern shore side, a new marina is proposed.

(For a detailed appraisal of the growth of vehicle ferry developments at Dover Eastern Docks, see the author's 'Ferry Port Dover' – available from Ferry Publications.)

CALAIS

The railway system in northern France was slower to develop than that in south east England. Although the railway had arrived at Calais in 1848 it did not offer a direct link with Paris but arrived via Lille – a distance of 235 miles. In the following year, the line was extended to the harbour where the first wooden maritime station was opened in August, being known to all as the 'Paradise' station. Illuminated by gaslight, it boasted a waiting hall which was 100 metres long and 20 metres wide.

Boulogne was not directly linked with Paris until 1851 which brought the years of plenty for the Folkestone route. Passengers preferred crossing from there rather than travelling on to Calais as the line from Paris via Lille took much longer. Once the direct Paris - Boulogne – Calais line was opened in 1867 (a distance of 168 miles), the Calais – Dover route again asserted its superiority and the South Eastern's service suffered as a result.

The lack of development at Calais in the mid-nineteenth century saw both the route suffer at the hands of the rival link between Folkestone and Boulogne and the requirement of the London Chatham & Dover Railway to retain their smaller steamers in order to offer passengers a service which could negotiate the shallows of the French port at all states of the tide.

A deep water berth was finally constructed at Calais and brought into use in August 1867 thus enabling vessels to dock whatever the tidal conditions. By fortune - or was it design? - it was commissioned just in time for the Paris World Fair and boasted a modest waiting room for passengers and customs formalities. The new terminal quickly gained approval and became so popular that it was frequently found wanting at busy periods. Rather than offering two termini in different parts of the harbour, plans were then set in motion to construct a new and single maritime station which was capable of handling all the traffic on offer.

With work starting on a new harbour in 1887, facilities were greatly improved and on 3rd June 1889, the President of France opened both it and the magnificently proportioned Gare Maritime which was to gain fame all over Europe for its superb cuisine. The new station was over 275 metres long and included railway offices, homes for seven officials, and a large hotel with attendant restaurant. There was still much dredging to

complete before Calais could safely accept the larger steamers at low water and it was not until 1895 that work was finally completed. Further improvements to the Gare Maritime were put in hand during 1938 – 39 but the advent of World War II saw work halted. Sadly the station became a victim of hostilities and was severely damaged during the conflict.

By the time that Calais was liberated, there was very little left of the Gare Maritime but a temporary terminal was constructed in time for the restoration of cross-Channel services in April 1946. Rebuilding of a permanent structure commenced almost immediately although the new red brick station was not officially opened until September 1959.

Just as with the 'Marine' station at Dover, the advent of car ferry traffic and the ending of the train-connected services in preparation for the opening of the Channel Tunnel saw the Gare Maritime close on 21st January 1995 although the building exists today for the benefit of lorry drivers rather than for train passengers.

Drive on – drive off facilities were used by the *Halladale* as from 1st July 1951 using the converted Callender-Hamilton bridge which Captain Townsend had bought from Yorkshire in 1946. It was placed at berth 3 and in 1965, the *Free Enterprise II* opened an adjacent linkspan at berth 4. Later still a third linkspan was built at number 2 berth right in front of the Gare Maritime and the three berths easily handled the traffic on Townsend's Dover service and the British Rail/SNCF links from both Dover and Folkestone. The railway ships still carried huge numbers of rail-connected passengers and even though their swinging area was somewhat restricted, easy access to the waiting Boat Trains was considered vital.

However, the impending arrival of the *Spirit of Free Enterprise* trio in 1980 required wider, deeper and longer berths and more room in which to manoeuvre. In preparation for their arrival, the Calais Chamber of Commerce embarked on the construction of a completely new port and the reclamation of large areas for vehicle parking. Berth 5 was built in the sand dunes to the north of the original berths which were all adjacent to Calais Maritime railway station. The freight section was commissioned on 17th April and one week later, the fine new terminal building was

The SNCF car ferry **Compiegne** *alongside at Calais Maritime with a 'Pacific' class locomotive ready to haul its Paris-bound train as far as Amiens. (John Hendy collection)*

Calais as seen from the freighter **European Seaway** *in August 1999 with the* **SeaFrance Nord Pas-de-Calais** *astern, the* **P&OSL Dover** *in berth 8 and the* **P&OSL Aquitaine** *leaving for Dover. (John Hendy)*

opened. Four more linkspans were subsequently constructed to the east of berth 5 with berth 9 being opened late in 2005. Berth 5 was rebuilt to handle larger ferries on the completion of berth 8 in 1995 while the older and smaller berths (numbers 2, 3 and 4) were later closed and removed. The Hoverspeed SeaCat berth was even further east and at the far end of the basin, just across the dunes from the Calais hoverport.

A lesser known cross-Channel service was operated from Calais and is briefly worth mentioning. The area on which the present day vehicle ferry berths are built was previously a lake which in 1912 was used by seaplanes. However, in 1928 a French company commenced a seaplane link to Dover using a bright yellow craft called the 'Canary'. A second craft was rather larger and crossed the Channel in 15 minutes. Facilities at Calais were good but at Dover the seaplanes had to land in the centre of the harbour and tie up to a buoy. Travellers were taken ashore in a motor boat which was uncomfortable and frequently took as long to reach land as had the entire crossing of the Dover Strait. Popularity waned and the service closed in 1934.

Plans are also afoot to create a completely new ferry port on the seaward side of the present harbour. Calais Port 2015 involves the building of four new linkspans in addition to new cruise and cargo handling facilities.

POST SCRIPT

The future of the Short-Sea Route between Dover and Calais is assured; new linkspans will be larger and the ferries that use them will reflect this. On board facilities have improved in terms of overall comfort and passenger requirements and the type of traffic now using the route

has undergone a complete revolution which has been led by the expectations and demands of the freight industry. Gone are the Atlantic liners in miniature with their magnificent lines which in themselves spoke volumes concerning man's constant struggle with the sea; the urgency involved in meeting the Continental Boat Expresses drawn up on the quaysides awaiting their cargoes of passengers and the Royal Mail; the Captains taking their diminutive ships out between the granite piers in all weathers, tide and sea states without stabilisers, radar, global positioning systems, ship to shore communications, bow-thrusters or variable-pitch propellers – simply using their expertise, skill and seamanship to reach their safe haven.

This book has aimed to capture something of the essence of the route's long and fascinating history and the many ships which have plied the 22-mile sea-lane.

Spending his formative years in post-war Dover, the comings and goings of the cross-Channel ships have provided the writer with a life long source of interest, study and pleasure. At one time there were no books available to his enquiring mind and so at the age of 18, he started producing them himself. This present publication is therefore one of a number which have been written about the port and its ferry-based activity and more are planned for the future.

For this writer, whenever he thinks of the Dover – Calais link, his mind immediately returns to the turbine steamship *Invicta* which reigned supreme on the daily 'Golden Arrow' link between 1946 and 1972. How different life was during that era and how thankful he is to have seen and witnessed it for himself.

Happy days indeed!

FLEET LIST

Note: Many of the early steamers listed below were also engaged on other routes from Dover and Folkestone to Boulogne, Calais, Ostend and elsewhere. Their Dover - Calais workings therefore formed only part of their schedules and detailed histories are often unclear. The SE&CR, Southern Railway and British Railways/ SNCF fleets also served Folkestone - Boulogne and later Dover - Boulogne while Townsend/ P&O ships also served Boulogne between 1986 - 1993 and Zeebrugge between 1966 -2002.

Name	Built	Builders	Gross Tons	Passengers	Cars	Service at Dover & Notes
BOYD (OF DOVER)						
Rob Roy	1818	Archibald, MacLachlan & Co, Dumbarton	90			1821. Sold to French PO 1822.
W BUSHELL (OF DOVER)						
Medusa	1822	Evans, Rotherhithe	94			1823-1837.Broken up.
Ondine	1845	Miller, Ravenhill & Co, Blackwall	86			1845-1847. Sold to Admiralty in 1847 and renamed *Undine*. 1854: purchased by Churchward and renamed *Dover*. Lost off Ostend in 1855.
J&W HAYWARD (OF DOVER)						
Sovereign	1822	James Duke, Dover	100			1822-1837. Sold to London owners.
Royal George	1826	James Duke, Dover	94			1826-1853. Sold locally.
Waterwitch	1835	Graham, Harwich	73			1836-1845. Sold to Poole owners.
Princess Alice	1843	Ditchburn & Mare, Blackwall	270			1843-1855. Sold to Devonport owners.
THE POST OFFICE						
Dasher	1821	Patterson, Rotherhithe	130			1821-1825. Wrecked Portpatrick 1830.
Arrow	1821	Evans, Rotherhithe	149			1822-1851. Taken over by Admiralty 1837, renamed *Ariel*.
Spitfire	1824	Graham, Harwich	111			1824-? Replaced *Dasher*.
Fury	1824	Graham, Harwich	112			1824-1828.Transferred to Margate-Ostend service.
Salamander	1827	Graham, Harwich	110			1827-c1845. Renamed *Beaver* by Admiralty in 1837.
Crusader	1827	Graham, Harwich	110			1827-1847. Renamed *Charon* by Admiralty in 1837.
Firefly	1831	Fletcher & Fearnall, Limehouse	100			1831-1848. Renamed *Myrtle* by Admiralty in 1837.
Ferret	1831	Pitcher, Blackwall	110			1831-1846. Renamed *Swallow* by Admiralty in 1837.
THE ADMIRALTY (FROM 1837)						
Widgeon	1837	Chatham Naval Dockyard	164			1837-1846. Became survey ship.
Dover	1840	Laird, Birkenhead	224			1840-1847. First iron steam ship in RN.
Onyx	1845	Ditchburn & Mare, Blackwall	294			1845- ?Replaced *Ariel*. Sold to Churchward 1854. Rebuilt and renamed *Vivid*. Taken over by LC&DR - chartered to French in 1871 when renamed *Scout*. Renamed *Vivid* on return to LC&DR.
Violet	1846	Ditchburn & Mare, Blackwall	295			1846-1857.Lost on Goodwins 1857.

DOVER CALAIS

Name	Built	Builders	Gross Tons	Passengers	Cars	Service at Dover & Notes
Garland	1846	Fletcher & Fearnall, Limehouse	295			1846-1864. Sold to Churchward in 1855. In 1856 renamed *L'Alliance* to carry French mails. Sold to LC&DR in 1862. Sold to Confederate States of America in 1864.
Vivid	1848	Chatham Naval Dockyard	352			1848-c1891.

SOUTH EASTERN & CONTINENTAL STEAM PACKET CO (FROM 1845) SOUTH EASTERN RAILWAY (FROM 1853-62)

Name	Built	Builders	Gross Tons	Passengers	Cars	Service at Dover & Notes
Princess Mary	1844	Ditchburn & Mare, Blackwall	109			1844-1846. In service at Folkestone until 1874.
CW Eborall	1882	Earle's, Hull	452			1899-1924. Cargo ship.
Achille Adam	1887	Samuda Bros, Poplar	460			1899-1914. Cargo ship. Sunk by *UB39* in March 1917.

JOSEPH CHURCHWARD (FROM 1853)

Name	Built	Builders	Gross Tons	Passengers	Cars	Service at Dover & Notes
Ondine	1847	Miller, Ravenhill & Co, Blackwall	171			1854-1862. Originally built to carry despatches. Sold to Churchward in 1854 but too slow. Sold for excursion work, then to Stornoway, Bristol and London. Broken up in 1889.
Queen	1855	CJ Mare, Blackwall	124			1855-c1865. Sold to France in 1855, renamed *La Reine*. Repurchased by LC&DR in 1865, renamed *Queen* - converted to cargo boat and latterly named *Pioneer*.
Empress	1855	CJ Mare, Blackwall	124			1855-c1865. Sold to France in 1855, renamed *L'Imperatrice*. Repurchased by LC&DR in 1865 and converted to cargo vessel being renamed *Pathfinder*.
Prince Frederick William	1857	Thames Ironworks, Blackwall	215			1857-1878. To LC&DR in 1862.
John Penn	1860	Thames Ironworks, Blackwall	203			1860-1862. Sold to Belgian Gov't for Ostend - Dover service, renamed *Perle*. Sold to France 1872: briefly returned to Calais mail service.
Jupiter	1849	Miller, Ravenhill, Blackwall	145			1856-1864. Built for service on Thames. Purchased by Churchward 1856. To LC&DR in 1862. Sold to Confederate States of America in 1864 but sank in Bay of Biscay.

ENGLISH CHANNEL STEAM SHIP CO/ ENGLISH CHANNEL TRANSIT CO

Name	Built	Builders	Gross Tons	Passengers	Cars	Service at Dover & Notes
Castalia	1874	Thames Ironworks, Blackwall	1,533			1874-1876. Sold 1883 and converted to hospital on Thames.
Express	1877	Leslie, Hebburn-on-Tyne	1,925			1877-1888. Taken over by LC&DR and renamed *Calais-Douvres*.

HENRY BESSEMER

Name	Built	Builders	Gross Tons	Passengers	Cars	Service at Dover & Notes
Bessemer	1874	Earle's, Hull	1,947			1875. Hull later rebuilt for conventional use.

LONDON CHATHAM & DOVER RAILWAY (TOOK OVER CHURCHWARD'S FLEET IN 1862)

Name	Built	Builders	Gross Tons	Passengers	Cars	Service at Dover & Notes
Samphire	1861	Money, Wigram, Blackwall	330			1862-1898. First local ship fitted with private cabins.
Maid of Kent	1861	Samuda Bros, Poplar	335			1862-1899.
Petrel	1862	Money, Wigram, Blackwall	503			1862-c1900. Fitted with a bow rudder.

This 2008 image shows the former SNCF car ferry **Compiegne**, *fifty years after entering service at Calais. Seen at Alexandria as the* **Al Ameerah**, *the vessel looks ready for the scrap yard. (John Wilson)*

The **Horsa** *operates as the* **Penelope A** *from Rafina (the second port of Athens) to the islands of Andros, Tinos and Mykonos. (John Hendy)*

Name	Built	Builders	Gross Tons	Passengers	Cars	Service at Dover & Notes
Scud	1862	Samuda Bros, Poplar	482			1862-1872. Sold to Canadian owners
Foam	1862	Samuda Bros, Poplar	497			1862-1901.
Breeze	1863	Money, Wigram, Blackwall	349			1863-c1900.
Wave	1863	Money, Wigram, Blackwall	344			1863-1899.
Prince Imperial	1864	James Ash, Poplar	327			1864-1899. Renamed *Prince* following the fall of the Second French Empire in 1872.
La France	1865	James Ash, Poplar	388			1865-1896.
Chatham	1873	Dudgeon, London	278			1873-1899. Cargo ship.
Calais	1874	Dudgeon, London	299			1874-1900. Cargo ship. Sold and renamed *Roubaix*, resold to London, Brighton & South Coast Railway (LB&SCR) in 1901, renamed *Trouville*. Scrapped 1911.
Paris	1878	Scott, Greenock	330			1878-1901. Sold to LB&SCR in 1901 and renamed *Calvados*. Scrapped 1911.
Invicta	1882	Thames Ironworks	1,236			1882-1899. Last local ship built on the Thames.
Victoria	1886	Fairfield, Govan	1,030			1886-1905.
Empress	1887	Fairfield, Govan	1,213			1887-1905.
Calais-Douvres	1889	Fairfield, Govan	1,212			1889-1900. First Channel steamer to be lit by electricity. Sold to Liverpool & Douglas Steamers Ltd then to Isle of Man Steam Packet Co in 1903. Renamed *Mona*. Scrapped 1909.
Dover	1896	Denny, Dumbarton	1,003			1896-1910. Scrapped 1911.
Calais	1896	Denny, Dumbarton	1,003			1896-1911. Sold French owners: renamed *Au Revoir* for tender service at Boulogne. Sunk by *U18* in February 1916.
Lord Warden	1896	Denny, Dumbarton	1,003			1896-1910. Scrapped 1911.

SOUTH EASTERN & CHATHAM RAILWAYS' JOINT MANAGING COMMITTEE (SE&CR) (FROM 1899)

Name	Built	Builders	Gross Tons	Passengers	Cars	Service at Dover & Notes
Maidstone	1899	Denny, Dumbarton	539			1899-1925. Cargo ship.
Canterbury	1901	Denny, Dumbarton	561	30		1901-1927. Cargo ship.
Walmer	1894	Denny, Dumbarton	513			1901-1938. Cargo ship. ex *Trouville* from LB&SCR.
Deal	1896	Denny, Dumbarton	572			1901-1926. Cargo ship ex *Prince Arthur* from LB&SCR.
Folkestone	1903	Denny, Dumbarton	496			1903-1927. Cargo ship.
The Queen	1903	Denny, Dumbarton	1,676			1903-1916. First cross-Channel turbine steamer. Sunk off Folkestone in August 1916.
Hythe	1905	Denny, Dumbarton	599			1905-1915. Cargo ship, sunk Dardanelles.
Onward	1905	Denny, Dumbarton	1,671			1905-1918. Sank at Folkestone Pier in 1918. Sold to Isle of Man Steam Packet Company: renamed *Mona's Isle*. Scrapped 1948.
Invicta	1905	Denny, Dumbarton	1,671			1905-1933. Sold to SAGA in 1923. Scrapped 1933.
Victoria	1907	Denny, Dumbarton	1,671			1907-1928. Sold to Isle of Man Steam Packet Company. Scrapped 1957.
Empress	1907	Denny, Dumbarton	1,671			1907-1933. Sold to SAGA in 1923. Scrapped 1933.
Riviera	1911	Denny, Dumbarton	1,675			1911-1932. Sold to Burns & Laird; renamed *Laird's Isle*. Scrapped in 1957.
Engadine	1911	Denny, Dumbarton	1,675			1911-1933. Sold to Philippines: renamed *Corregidor*. Sank in Manila Bay December 1941.
Biarritz	1915	Denny, Dumbarton	2,388			1921-1939. Scrapped at Dover in 1950

*The former **Hengist** of 1972 as she appeared during 2008. As the **Agios Georgios**, the ferry maintains a tough daily schedule from Piraeus to the island of Milos. She is seen here at Sifnos. (John Hendy)*

*After closing the Calais - Dover train-connected service in September 1993, the **Chartres** was sold to Greece where she became the **Express Santorini** running to the island whose name she bore. This finished in 2006 and during 2007-8, she was chartered for summer use in the Azores. (John Hendy)*

DOVER
CALAIS

After closing the Newhaven - Dieppe route, the **Stena Cambria** *(ex* **St. Anselm***) was sold to Spanish owners in 1999 and renamed* **Isla de Botafoc***. (Bruce Peter)*

The **Express Milos** *was the former* **Vortigern** *and served in Greece for 17 years before being broken up in 2005. (Miles Cowsill)*

Name	Built	Builders	Gross Tons	Passengers	Cars	Service at Dover & Notes
Maid of Orleans	1918	Denny, Dumbarton	2,384			1920-1939. Sank off Normandy Beaches June 1944.

SOUTHERN RAILWAY CO (FROM 1923)

Name	Built	Builders	Gross Tons	Passengers	Cars	Service at Dover & Notes
Tonbridge	1924	Henderson, Port Glasgow	682			1924-1939. Cargo ship. Sunk off Yarmouth August 1941.
Minster	1924	Henderson, Port Glasgow	682			1924-1939. Cargo ship. Transferred to Southampton 1936. Sunk off Normandy June 1944.
Hythe	1925	Henderson, Port Glasgow	685			1925-1949. Cargo ship: to Southampton in 1949. Scrapped at Dover 1956.
Whitstable	1925	Henderson, Port Glasgow	687			1925-1948. Cargo ship: to Southampton in 1948. Scrapped 1959.
Isle of Thanet	1925	Denny, Dumbarton	2,701	1,400		1925-1963. Scrapped 1964.
Maid of Kent	1925	Denny, Dumbarton	2,701	1,400		1925-1939. Bombed and sunk at Dieppe, May 1940.
Maidstone	1926	Henderson, Port Glasgow	688			1926-1953. Cargo ship: to Heysham in 1953. Scrapped 1958.
Deal	1928	Henderson, Port Glasgow	688			1928-1947. Cargo ship. Scrapped 1963. Post war: Folkestone-Boulogne.
Canterbury	1929	Denny, Dumbarton	2,910	1,400		1929-1964. 'Golden Arrow' steamer. Scrapped 1965.
Autocarrier	1931	Henderson, Port Glasgow	822	307	26	1931-1954. Route's first purpose-built car ferry. Scrapped 1954.
Invicta	1940	Denny, Dumbarton	4,178	1,400		1946-1972. 'Golden Arrow' steamer. Scrapped 1972.

BRITISH TRANSPORT COMMISSION
BRITISH RAILWAYS (SOUTHERN REGION) (FROM 1948)
BRITISH RAIL (FROM 1964)
BRITISH RAILWAYS SHIPPING & INTERNATIONAL SERVICES DIVISION (1968 - TRADING AS SEALINK FROM 1970)
SEALINK UK LTD (FROM 1979)

Name	Built	Builders	Gross Tons	Passengers	Cars	Service at Dover & Notes
Maid of Orleans	1949	Denny, Dumbarton	3,777	1,400		1949-1975. Scrapped: 1975.
Lord Warden	1952	Denny, Dumbarton	3,333	1,000	120	1952-1978. Sold Saudi Arabia: renamed *Al Zaher*. Scrapped 1981.
Maid of Kent	1959	Denny, Dumbarton	3,920	1,000	180	1959-1974.Moved to Weymouth-Cherbourg. Scrapped 1981.
Normannia	1952	Denny, Dumbarton	2,219	500	111	1964-1978. Built for Southampton-Le Havre route. Converted to car ferry in 1964. Scrapped: 1978.
St Patrick	1948	Cammell Laird, Birkenhead	3,147	1,200		1964-1971. Weymouth-Channel Islands service until 1964. Sold Greece: renamed *Thermopylae* then *Agapitos 1*. Scrapped 1980.
Dover	1965	Swan Hunter, Wallsend	3,602	1,000	205	1965-1980. Converted to drive through in 1977: renamed *Earl Siward*. Sold to Cyprus: renamed *Sol Express*. In 1986 sold for nightclub use on Tyne and then Tees: renamed *Tuxedo Royale*. 2008 - laid up at Hartlepool.
Vortigern	1969	Swan Hunter, Wallsend	4,371	1,000	240	1969-1988. 'Multi-purpose' car and train ferry. Sold Greece 1988: renamed *Milos Express*, then *Express Milos*, then *Nisos Limnos*. Broken up 2005.

Name	Built	Builders	Gross Tons	Passengers	Cars	Service at Dover & Notes
Hengist	1972	Naval Dockyard, Brest	5,590	1,400	210	1972-1990. Renamed *Stena Hengist* in 1990.Sold Greece.in 1992 - renamed *Romilda*, then *Apollo Express II* in 1993, *Express Artemis* in 1999, *Panagia Ekatontapiliani* in 2001, *Agios Geogios* in 2004 Still in service 2009.
Horsa	1972	Naval Dockyard, Brest	5,590	1,400	210	1972-1991.Renamed *Stena Horsa* in 1990. Sold Greece.in 1992.Renamed *Penelope A*, then *Express Penelope* in 1999 and *Penelope A* in 2004. Still in service 2009.
Holyhead Ferry 1	1965	Hawthorn, Leslie, Newcastle	3,879	1,000	160	1973-1980. Built for Holyhead-Dun Laoghaire route but seasonally transferred to Dover from 1973. Converted to drive-through in 1976, renamed *Earl Leofric*. Scrapped 1981.
Caesarea	1960	JS White, Cowes	4,174	1,400		1976-1980. Built for Weymouth-Channel Islands route. Sold Hong Kong in 1980, broken up 1986.
St Anselm	1980	Harland & Wolff, Belfast	7,399	1,400	309	1980-1998. Renamed *Stena Cambria* in 1990 for service Holyhead-Dun Laoghaire. Regular returns to Dover. Closed Newhaven-Dieppe in 1999.Sold Spain. Still in service (2009) as *Isla de Botafoc*.
St Christopher	1981	Harland & Wolff, Belfast	7,399	1,400	309	1981-1991.Renamed *Stena Antrim* in 1990 for Stranraer-Larne route. Sold in 1998 to Moroccan owners: renamed *Ibn Batouta*. 2009: still in service.
Caledonian Princess	1961	Denny, Dumbarton	4,042	1,400	103	1981-1981. Built for Stranraer-Larne service. Came to Dover vice *Caesarea* in 1981. Sold as a nightclub at Gateshead: renamed *Tuxedo Princess*. Scrapped 2008.

SEA CONTAINERS, BERMUDA
SEALINK BRITISH FERRIES (FROM 1984)

Name	Built	Builders	Gross Tons	Passengers	Cars	Service at Dover & Notes
St. David	1981	Harland & Wolff, Belfast	7,179	1,154	309	1983-1985.Operated on Holyhead-Dun Laoghaire. Transferred to Dover - Ostend service. 2009 still in service Stranraer-Belfast as the *Stena Caledonia*.
Fantasia	1980	Kockums Varv, Malmo	25,243	1,800	723	1990-2003. Built as deep-sea ro-ro vessel *Scandinavia*. Renamed *Tzarevetz* (1982), then *Fiesta* (1988).Rebuilt 1989-90. Renamed *Stena Fantasia* in 1990, then *P&OSL Canterbury* in 1998 and *PO Canterbury* in 2002. Sold Greece in 2004 renamed *Alkmini A*. Sold Poland 2004, renamed *Wawel*; 2009: in service.
Saint Eloi	1975	Cantieri Navali,Genoa, Italy	4,649	1,000	160	1988-1989.Train ferry replaced on Dover-Dunkirk service in 1988 Retained to operate summer train-connected services. Chartered by SNCF during summer 1988 but renamed *Channel Entente* with British management in 1989. Sold to Isle of Man Steam Packet Co in 1990, renamed *King Orry*. Sold Italy in 1998 renamed *Moby Love 2* then *Moby Love*, then *Moby Love 2*. 2009: still in service.

STENA LINE SWEDEN
SEALINK STENA LINE (FROM 1990)
STENA SEALINK LINE (FROM 1992)
STENA LINE (FROM 1996)

Name	Built	Builders	Gross Tons	Passengers	Cars	Service at Dover & Notes
Stena Invicta	1985	Nakskov, Denmark	19,763	2,000	430	1991-1998. Built as *Pedar Paars* for Danish internal service. 1998: Chartered then sold and renamed *Color Viking*. In service 2009.
Stena Challenger	1991	Bruces Verkstad, Landskrona	18,523	500	480	1991-1996. Transferred to Irish Sea. Sold to Canada 2000, renamed *Leif Ericson*. In service 2009.
Stena Empereur	1983	Chantiers du Nord, Dunkirk	28,559	2,036	550	1996-2004. Built as *Stena Jutlandica*. Became *P&OSL Provence* in 1998, *PO Provence* in 2002 and *Pride of Provence* in 2003. Sold to Greece in 2004 renamed *Alkmini A*. Chartered and later sold Norway 2005, renamed *Pride of Telemark*. Laid up 2008.

TOWNSEND BROS CAR FERRIES LTD (1928)
GEORGE NOTT INDUSTRIES (1956)
TRADING AS TOWNSEND CAR FERRIES (FROM 1965)
PART OF THE EUROPEAN FERRIES GROUP (1968)
TRADING AS TOWNSEND THORESEN FERRIES (FROM 1976)

Name	Built	Builders	Gross Tons	Passengers	Cars	Service at Dover & Notes
Forde	1919	Dunlop, Bremner, Port Glasgow	829	307	28	1930-1949. Built as HMS *Ford*, a 'Town' class minesweeper. Sold Gibraltar 1949 and renamed *Gibel Tarik*. Scrapped 1954.
Halladale	1944	A&J Inglis, Pointhouse, Glasgow	1,370	388	55	1950-1961. Built as HMS *Halladale*, a 'River' class frigate.Sold to Finland in 1961: renamed *Norden* then *Turist Expressen*. 1962 - sold to Venezuela and renamed *Ferrymar III*. Hulk scrapped 1987.
Free Enterprise	1960	NV Werf 'Gusto', Schiedam	2,607	850	120	1962-1980. Renamed *Free Enterprise I* in 1965. Sold Greece 1981 and renamed *Kimolos*, then *Ergina* in 1993, then *Methodia II* in 1995, then *Kallisti* in 1997, then *Okeanis* in 2005. 2008:laid-up.
Free Enterprise II	1965	NV Werf 'Gusto', Schiedam	4,011	998	205	1965-1980. Sold Italy. Renamed *Moby Blu*. Scrapped 2003.
Free Enterprise III	1966	NV Werf 'Gusto'; Schiedam	4,657	1,114	221	1966-1981. Sold 1984 to Malta: renamed *Tamira*. Sold 1984 Isle of Man Steam Packet Co: renamed *Mona's Isle*. Sold 1986 to Egypt: renamed *Al Fahad*. 1994: abandoned near Jeddah.
Free Enterprise IV	1969	NV Werf 'Gusto', Schiedam	5,049	1,132	260	1969-1988. Sold to Danish owners: renamed *Falster Link*. Sold to Egypt 1998: renamed *Tag Al Salam*. Scrapped 2006.
Free Enterprise V	1970	NV Werf 'Gusto', Schiedam	5,044	1,132	260	1970-1993. Renamed *Pride of Hythe* in 1987. Sold 1993 to Slovenian owners: renamed *Laburnum*. 2003: renamed *Tadla*. 2007: renamed *Veronica Line*. 2008: in service.
Free Enterprise VI	1972	NV Werf 'Gusto', Schiedam	4,981	1,132	314	1972-1992. Renamed *Pride of Sandwich* in 1987. Rebuilt: 1985. Transferred to North Channel in 1992, renamed *Pride of Ailsa*. Sold to Egypt 1996: renamed *Pride of Al Salam 95*. Rammed and sunk 2005.

Still instantly recognisable as the **Free Enterprise**, *Townsend's ground-breaking car ferry has served in Greek waters for longer than she did in the Dover Strait but is presently (2009) laid-up at Elefsis. (Miles Cowsill)*

The last of the 'Free Enterprises,' the **Free Enterprise VIII/ Pride of Canterbury** *today operates as the* **Romilda** *on her owners' service to Rhodes. (Miles Cowsill)*

Name	Built	Builders	Gross Tons	Passengers	Cars	Service at Dover & Notes
Free Enterprise VII	1973	NV Werf 'Gusto', Schiedam	4,981	1,132	314	1973-1992. Renamed *Pride of Walmer* in 1987. Rebuilt 1986. Transferred to North Channel 1992: renamed *Pride of Rathlin*. Sold 2000 to Indonesia: renamed *BSP III*. 2009: in service.
Free Enterprise VIII	1974	Verolme, Alblasserdam	5,170	1,101	320	1974-1993. Renamed *Pride of Canterbury* in 1987. Sold Greece 1993: renamed *Romilda*. 2009: in service.
European Trader	1975	SUAG, Bremerhaven	3,335	132	76 lorries	1975-1991. Sold 2001, became *Taygran Trader*, sold Egypt 2001, renamed *Lina Trader*. Scrapped 2006.
European Clearway	1975	SUAG, Bremerhaven	3,335	132	76 lorries	1975-1992. Renamed *Panther* 1996, renamed *European Pathfinder* 1998, Sold Greece 2002, renamed *Regina I*, resold to Slovenian owners 2002, renamed *Begonia*. Resold Estonia 2005, renamed *Via Mare*. 2009: still in service.
European Enterprise	1978	SUAG, Bremerhaven	3,767	132	76 lorries	1978-1995. Renamed *European Endeavour* in 1987, sold 2002 to Slovenian owners and renamed *Gardenia*. 2009: still in service.
Spirit of Free Enterprise	1980	SUAG, Bremerhaven	7,951	1,300	350	1980-2003. Renamed *Pride of Kent* in 1987 then *P&OSL Kent* in 1998. Became *PO Kent* in 2002. Sold Greek owners: renamed *Anthi Marina*. 2009: in service.
Herald of Free Enterprise	1980	SUAG, Bremerhaven	7,951	1,300	50	1980-1987. Lost off Zeebrugge with 193 passengers and crew 1987.
Pride of Enterprise	1980	SUAG, Bremerhaven	7,951	1,300	350	1980-2000. Renamed *Pride of Free Bruges* in 1987 then *P&OSL Picardy* in 1998. Sold Slovenian owners in 2001, named *Oleander*. 2009: in service
Pride of Dover	1987	SUAG, Bremen	26,433	2,290	650	1987-. Renamed *P&OSL Dover* in 1998 then *PO Dover* in 2002 and *Pride of Dover* in 2003. 2009: in service.
Pride of Calais	1987	SUAG, Bremen	26,433	2,290	650	1987-. Renamed *P&OSL Calais* in 1998 then *PO Calais* in 2002 and *Pride of Calais* in 2003. 2009: in service.

P&O EUROPEAN FERRIES (FROM 1987)

Name	Built	Builders	Gross Tons	Passengers	Cars	Service at Dover & Notes
European Seaway	1991	Seebeckwerft, Bremerhaven	22,986	200	124 lorries	1991. Built mainly for Zeebrugge freight but on Calais route since 2003. 2009: in service.
European Pathway	1991	Seebeckwerft, Bremerhaven	22,986	200	124 lorries	1991. Rebuilt and renamed *Pride of Canterbury* in 2003.
European Highway	1991	Seebeckweft, Bremerhaven	22,986	200	124 lorries	1991. Rebuilt and renamed *Pride of Kent* in 2003.
Pride of Burgundy	1992	Seebeckwerft, Bremerhaven	28,138	1,420	600	1992. Renamed *P&OSL Burgundy* in 1998 then *PO Burgundy* in 2002 and *Pride of Burgundy* in 2003. 2009: Still in service.

P&O STENA LINE   (FROM 1998)

Name	Built	Builders	Gross Tons	Passengers	Cars	Service at Dover & Notes
P&OSL Aquitaine	1992	Boelwerf, Temse, Belgium	28,883	1,400	710	1998-2005. Built for Ostend - Dover service as *Prins Filip*. UK base to Ramsgate 1994. Service closed 1997. 1998: renamed *Stena Royal* and chartered to P&O Stena Line and became *P&OSL Aquitaine*. 2002: *PO Aquitaine*. 2003: *Pride of Aquitaine*. Charter ended 2005. Became *Norman Spirit* for LD Lines. In service 2009.

P&O FERRIES (FROM 2002)

Name	Built	Builders	Gross Tons	Passengers	Cars	Service at Dover & Notes
Pride of Canterbury	rebuilt 2003		30,365	2,000	650	2003-. ex *European Pathway* In service 2009.
Pride of Kent	rebuilt 2003		30,365	2,000	650	2003. ex *European Highway* In service 2009.
European Endeavour	2000	AESA, Seville, Spain	22,152	214	144 lorries	2008. Built as *Midnight Merchant*. Dover - Dunkirk until 2006. Then Spanish charter:renamed *El Greco*. Purchased by P&O in 2007. In service 2009.
New building 1	2010	STX Europe, Finland	49,000	2,000	180 lorries+195 cars.	
New building 2	2011	STX Europe, Finland	49,000	2,000	180 lorries+195 cars.	

FRENCH OPERATORS

FRENCH POST OFFICE (1822-1855)
CHEMIN DE FER DU NORD (FROM 1898)
SAGA (FROM 1920)
SNCF (FROM 1938)
SEALINK SNAT (FROM 1990)
SEAFRANCE (FROM 1996)

Name	Built	Builders	Gross Tons	Passengers	Cars	Notes
Henri Quatre	1818	Archibald, MacLachlan, Dumbarton	90			1822-c1830. ex *Rob Roy*. Sold to French Post Office in 1822. Renamed *Henri Quatre*, 1824 *Duc d'Orleans*.
Duc de Bordeaux	1824	France				1824-1831. Renamed *Jeune France* in 1830. Sold 1831.
Courrier	1830	Normand, Le Havre				1830-c1845. Sold c1845.
Poste	1834	Cherbourg				1834-1848.
Estafette	1834	Cherbourg				1834-1848.
Daim	1848	Bordeaux				1848-1855. Sold when French lost mail contract to Churchward.
La Biche	1848	Bordeaux				1848-1855.
Le Faon	1847	Normand, Le Havre				1847-1855.
Honfleur	18 __					1847-1855.
Le Nord	1898	Chantiers de la Loire, St Nazaire	2,004			1898-1923. Ownership to SAGA: 1920. Scrapped 1923.
Le Pas-de-Calais	1898	Chantiers de la Loire, St Nazaire	2,004			1898-1923. Ownership to SAGA: 1920. Scrapped 1923.
Cote d'Azur	1930	Ch. de la Mediterranee, Le Havre	3.047			1931-1939. Bombed at Dunkirk 1940. Raised and renamed *Elsass* but mined and sunk in January 1945.
Cote d'Argent	1932	Ch. de la Mediterranee, Le Havre	3,047			1933-1939. Captured by Germans, Cherbourg 1940. Renamed *Ostmark* - sunk by RAF in April 1945.
Compiegne	1958	Loire-Normandie, Rouen	3,467	1,000	164	1958-1981. Sold Greece: renamed *Ionian Glory*, resold 1989 renamed *Queen Vergina*, resold 1990: renamed *Freedom 1*, resold 1994 renamed *Katerina*, resold 1995 renamed *Al Amira*, then *Al Ameerah*.
Chantilly	1966	Dubigeon-Normandie, Nantes	3,255	1,350	200	1966-1984. 1975-76 - converted to drive through.1985 - switched to Dieppe-Newhaven. 1987: sold Greece and renamed *Olympia*. 1990: became *Europa Link* (Denmark-Germany), 1993: sold Poland and became *Baltavia*. 1996: sold Egypt and became *El Salam 93*. Scrapped.
Chartres	1974	Dubigeon-Normandie, Nantes	4,590	1,400	240	1974-1993. Multi-purpose train/ vehicle ferry. 1982-89: Dieppe - Newhaven. Returned to Calais 1990-93. Sold Greece and renamed *Express Santorini*. Laid up late 2008.

The **Pride of Free Enterprise/ Pride of Bruges/ Pride of Picardy** *was sold to Slovenian operators TransEuropa Ferries in 2001 and renamed* **Oleander**. *She operates between Ostend and Ramsgate. (John Hendy)*

The **Spirit of Free Enterprise/ Pride of Kent** *was sold to Greece in 2003 and renamed* **Anthi Marina** *for service between Piraeus and Rhodes. (John Hendy)*

Name	Built	Builders	Gross Tons	Passengers	Cars	Service at Dover & Notes
Cote d'Azur	1981	Ateliers et Chantiers du Havre	8,862	1,596	330	1981-2009. Renamed *SeaFrance Renoir* in 1996. In service 2009.
Champs Elysees	1984	Dubigeon Normandie, Nantes	9,069	1,800	330	1984-2008. Switched to Dieppe 1990, 1992: chartered by Stena and renamed *Stena Parisien*. 1997: returned to Calais and renamed *SeaFrance Manet*. Laid up 2008.
Fiesta	1980	Kockums Varv, Malmo	25,122	1,800	640	1990-2009. Built as deep sea ro-ro vessel *Ariadne* but renamed *Soca* (1990): sold 1991, became *Trapezitza*. 1998: Sold to Sea Containers and renamed *Fantasia* then freighter *Channel Seaway* on Dover-Calais in 1989. Rebuilt and became *Fiesta*. Renamed *SeaFrance Cezanne* in 1996.
Nord Pas-de-Calais	1987	Chantiers du Nord, Dunkirk	13,727	80	90 lorries	1987-. Built as Dunkirk train ferry 1996: received 'SeaFrance' prefix and returned to Calais-Dover freight runs. In service 2009.
SeaFrance Monet	1974	Trogir, Yugoslavia	6,737	1,800	425	Launched as *Stena Nordica* but renamed *Stena Danica* (1974) then *Stena Nordica* (1981), *Stena Nautica* (1984), *Versailles* (after sale to SNCF in1987), *Stena Londoner* (1992). To Calais in 1996 renamed *SeaFrance Monet*. Sold Spain 2000, renamed *Volcan de Tecande*. 2005: scrapped
SeaFrance Rodin	2001	Aker Finnyards, Finland	33,796	1,900	700	2001. In service 2009.
SeaFrance Berlioz	2004	Chantiers Atlantique, St Nazaire	33,796	1,900	700	2004. In service 2009.
SeaFrance Moliere	2002	Deutsche Werft, Kiel	30,285	1,200	480	2008. Built as Greek flag ferry *Superfast X*. Sold France 1996: renamed *Jean Nicoli*. Resold to SNCF 2007. In service 2009.

HOVERSPEED (FROM 1981)
FORMERLY HOVERLLOYD (RAMSGATE-CALAIS) AND THE BRITISH RAILWAYS' BOARD SUBSIDIARY, SEASPEED (DOVER-BOULOGNE) BUT MERGED TO FORM HOVERSPEED IN 1981; AN INDEPENDENT COMPANY FROM 1984; A SUBSIDIARY OF SEA CONTAINERS FROM 1986.

HOVERCRAFT

Name	Built	Builders		Passengers	Cars	Service at Dover & Notes
The Princess Margaret	1968	BHC, East Cowes		424	55	1968-2000. Laid up Lee-on-Solent.
Swift	1968	BHC, East Cowes		278	36	1981-1991. Scrapped at Lee-on-Solent in 2004.
The Princess Anne	1969	BHC, East Cowes		424	55	1969-2000. Laid up Lee-on-Solent.
Sir Christopher	1972	BHC, East Cowes		278	36	1981-1991. Scrapped 1998.
Prince of Wales	1977	BHC, East Cowes		278	36	1981-1991. Scrapped following fire 1993.
Ingenieur Jean-Bertin	1977	Sedam, Paullac, France		385	45	1977-1985. SNCF craft. Scrapped. 1985.

SEACATS (all served highly peripatetic careers but sometime worked on Dover-Calais during the period of their operation)

Name	Built	Builders	Gross Tons	Passengers	Cars	Service at Dover & Notes
Hoverspeed Great Britain	1990	InCat, Tasmania	3,000	577	80	Launched as *Christopher Columbus* (025). Sold to Greece 2005, renamed *Speedrunner 1*, sold 2008 *Sea Runner* (pass only).
Hoverspeed France	1991	InCat, Tasmania	3,003	450	80	1992 charter, renamed *Sardegna Express*. 1992: *SeaCat Boulogne*, 1994 *SeaCat Isle of Man*, 1996: *SeaCat Norge*, 1997: *SeaCat Isle of Man*, 2005: *Sea Express 1*, 2008: *Snaefell*.

*The freighter **European Enterprise/ European Endeavour** was also sold to TransEuropa Ferries and operates on the Ostend - Ramsgate link. As the **Gardenia**, the thirty-year old vessel very much represents an earlier age of ro-ro ship. (John Hendy)*

*The **Speedrunner 1 (ex Hoverspeed Great Britain)** pictured in the twilight of her career in Greece in September 2005. (John Hendy)*

Name	Built	Builders	Gross Tons	Passengers	Cars	Service at Dover & Notes
SeaCat Tasmania	1991	InCat, Tasmania	3,012	350	80	1993: *SeaCat Calais*, 1994: *Atlantic II* (charter), 2000: *Croazia Jet* (charter), 2002: *SeaCat France*, 2005: *Emeraude France* (charter) and then sold.
Hoverspeed Boulogne	1991	InCat, Tasmania	3,003	432	80	Launched as *Hoverspeed Belgium*. 1991: *Hoverspeed Boulogne*, 1993: *SeaCatamaran Danmark*, 1995: *SeaCat Danmark*, 2003: *Pescara Jet*.
SeaCat Scotland	1992	Incat, Tasmania	3,003	450	80	1994:*Q-Ship Express* (charter), 1995: *SeaCat Scotland*, 2007: *Shikra*.
Diamant	1996	InCat, Tasmania	3,454	654	140	1996: *Holyman Express*, 1997: *Holyman Diamant*, 1998 to Dover and renamed *Diamant*. 2004: *SeaCat Diamant* Sold to Spain 2007: renamed *Jaume III*.
Rapide	1996	InCat, Tasmania	3,454	654	140	1996: *Holyman Rapide*, 1998: to Dover and renamed *Rapide*. 2004 *SeaCat Rapide*, Sold to Spain 2006: renamed *Jaume II*.
SuperSeaCat One	1997	Fincantieri, Italy	4,662	782	175	2001: Sold to Spain and renamed *Almudaina Dos* in 2006.
SuperSeaCat Two	1997	Fincantieri, Italy	4,500	800	175	1997 & 2001: Renamed *Viking* for Isle of Man Steam Packet Co in 2008.
SuperSeaCat Three	1999	Fincantieri, Italy	4,465	782	175	2001: Sold Estonia, renamed *Tallink Autoexpress* in 2007.

ACKNOWLEDGEMENTS

The writer acknowledges the assistance of the following people and sources in connection with this publication: Andrew Jones, Bruce Peter (for access to AE Glen's collection), Ray Goodfellow and Nigel Thornton (www.doverferryphotos.co.uk), Timothy Cowsill for undertaking all the PhotoShop and scanning work, FotoFlite of Ashford, John Lewis at Gomer Press, P&O Ferries and SeaFrance for their support and to my colleague Miles Cowsill for his invaluable assistance in designing and publishing the book.

FURTHER READING

All available from Ferry Publications (www.ferrypubs.co.uk)

Ferry Port Dover (charting the port's car ferry development from 1928)

The Townsend Eight (the eight 'Free Enterprise' ships)

The Saints Go Marching On (the four Sealink 'Saint' class ships)

The Sealink Years (the year by year history of the famous ferry company)

Five Days in Greece (a 2005 visit to Greece catching up with former UK ferries)

P&O Ferries - The Fleet (a comprehensive history and illustrated fleet list)